For the Love of Coffee

Karen Rowe

First printed in 2009 10 9 8 7 6 5 4 3 2 1
Printed in Canada

The Publisher: Blue Bike Books
Website: www.bluebikebooks.com

Library and Archives Canada Cataloguing in Publication

Rowe, Karen, 1975–
For the love of coffee / by Karen Rowe.

Includes bibliographical references.

ISBN 978-1-897278-65-9

1. Coffee—Miscellanea. 2. Coffee drinking—Miscellanea. I. Title.
TX415.R69 2009641.3'373C2009-900172-1

Project Director: Nicholle Carrière
Project Editor: Jordan Allan
Cover Images: Photos.com
Illustrations: Craig Howrie
Photography Credits: Every effort has been made to accurately credit the sources of photographs. Any errors or omissions should be reported directly to the publisher for correction in future editions. Photographs courtesy of Photos.com (p. 19, p. 39, p. 41, p. 43, p. 45, p. 46, p. 77, p. 84, p. 118, p. 160, p. 189, p. 192, p. 197, p. 210, p. 218, p. 221, p. 229, p. 235, p. 240); Karen Rowe (p. 9, p. 72, p. 93, p. 145, p. 225)

We acknowledge the support of the Alberta Foundation for the Arts for our publishing program.

We acknowledge the financial support of the Government of Canada through the Book Publishing Industry Development Program (BPIDP) for our publishing activities.

Canadian Heritage   Patrimoine canadien

PC: 06

DEDICATION

To my sister Jane, with whom I have traveled so far—I would never have figured out how to work the espresso machine without you.

And to all you perky morning people out there—we know who you are!

CONTENTS

ACKNOWLEDGEMENTS

I would like to thank everyone who had anything to do with this book—with energy, intelligence and kindness you have each in your own ways guided me towards the path of clarity. Thank you for weaving a safety net of support beneath my tightrope.

Gratitude to my friend Jordan, who helped me break through a brick wall of writer's block, even if her help felt like she was piercing my ear with a potato in my parents' basement.

Thanks to my editor and publisher for their support, enthusiasm and enduring patience.

Also thanks to Sharon and Scott Evans, for some space and time in peace and quiet.

And to Craig and Echo, for all the years.

I raise my cup to you all.

INTRODUCTION

My dad always used to joke that he liked his coffee like he liked his women—lukewarm and indifferent. My mom thought this was the funniest thing she had ever heard, probably because she was the furthest you could get from lukewarm and indifferent. The joke is a reminder to me of my dad's sense of humour; it's from him that I get my love of puns.

On the other hand, I don't know where my love of coffee came from. I lived in France for a year and thought their coffee tasted like jet fuel—I hated it. But now, like most people, I can't imagine living without coffee.

Coffee is literally the lifeblood of the modern world. Its worldwide popularity is undeniable; without coffee, an entire range of businesses—from telemarketing to accounting to, well, *writing*—simply could not function.

Case in point—this book could not have been written without many cups of coffee.

It is a myth that money makes the world go round; coffee is the true mechanism that keeps the world in motion.

Coffee hasn't had an easy road, though. Over the past few centuries, it has been banned in almost every country and has been blamed for fueling riots, triggering sedition and leading to Satanic worship. Alright!

And like any good villain, coffee has been shrouded in mystery from its very first discovery, imbued with magical properties and surrounded with controversy. Legend links coffee with famous doctors, priests, poets and philosophers; scholars, artists, merchants and politicians; and pirates, swashbucklers, dancing goats and drug smugglers. The first coffee drinkers experienced sensations ranging from exhilaration to religious ecstasy—no wonder the beverage became so popular.

Across the years, many talented and dynamic individuals have dreamed of ushering in a new age over brimming cups in coffee houses in Constantinople, London and New York. They shaped history and became the leaders of their time. The coffee house has been everything from a pulpit and courtroom to a stage and classroom.

And centuries later, the brew helped fuel the industrial revolution, especially once factory managers learned that filling their workers with free coffee boosted their productivity. Coffee made people feel smarter, helped them do better work and enabled them to be on time every morning.

As any modern cubicle dweller—and writer—can confirm, coffee almost single-handedly makes everyday work possible. Today, coffee is the second most traded physical commodity in the world after petroleum. And whether you prefer the widespread corporate chains or the local independent coffee house, you're taking a step into a long history of coffee each time you stop for a latte.

So brew up a pot and enjoy this book; it's sure to keep you percolating.

ORIGINS

Beginnings

The English word "coffee" came into regular use in the early 1600s. It originated either from the Arabic word *qahwa*, via the Turkish word *kahve* and the Italian *caffè,* or from the name of the coffee-growing Kaffa region in western Ethiopia.

Coffee is now cultivated in more than 70 countries, mostly in the fertile region between the Tropic of Cancer and the Tropic of Capricorn. The so-named "Coffee Belt" straddles the equator by 30 degrees north and south. The landscape ranges from tropical forests to barren deserts, and the history of coffee is as rich and varied as the land in which it grows.

Caffeine may be the world's most popular drug, but as a drink it is relatively young. Although there are a few scattered references to coffee between 900 and 1000 AD, when it was initially prepared as a food, coffee as a beverage didn't really make its grand entrance until around 1500 AD.

Primitive Power Bar (Circa 800 AD)

Coffee beans are the seeds of a fruit similar to a cherry. African tribes would use stone mortars to grind the ripe coffee cherries, then mixed them with animal fat and rolled them into round balls that they carried with them as food in the desert. Raw coffee is extremely potent and has a high protein content, a benefit that is lost when it is prepared as a beverage. The animal fat and protein provided concentrated nourishment, while the considerable caffeine content of the mixture acted as a stimulant that spurred the African warriors on to, as the author of *The Book of Coffee & Tea* puts it, "heights of savagery."

The early beverage form of coffee first appeared as a wine made in Africa from the fermented juice of the ripe cherries mixed with cold water. In some cases, the aroma of the dried beans was so appealing that the Africans simply soaked the whole beans in water and drank the remains. It wasn't until later that they began crushing them.

Nature's Deodorant

A drink called *buncham*, brewed from the *bunn* plant, was consumed by the Ethiopians around the 11th century. *Buncham* is said to have been beneficial to the stomach and the skin and would sweat out through the pores, giving a sweet scent to the whole body. In the days before baths were regularly taken, this natural deodorant must have been like a breath of fresh air.

Hot Drink (Circa 1000 to 1600 AD)

The story of coffee as we know and crave it today begins in the country formerly known as Arabia, present-day Yemen. According to Jon Thorn, author of *The Coffee Companion*, the cultivation of coffee began in Yemen as early as 575 AD, although reports vary. Either way, we know we have the Arab world to thank for turning coffee into a hot beverage when they started boiling it in about 1000 AD.

Out of Africa

Everyone is in agreement about one thing: coffee originated in Ethiopia in the province of Kaffa. Where the tales and legends start differing is during coffee's transmission from Ethiopia, where it was harvested from the forest, to Arabia, where it was first cultivated. The most common theory is that coffee cherries, known as "magical fruit," were eaten by Sudanese slaves to help them on their long trek into Arabia. Some of the beans may have survived the journey and germinated. Reportedly, there is still a trail of coffee trees along the old Zambezi slave route to Beira in Mozambique. It is equally possible that the Arab slave traders simply brought the berries back with them on their return trips from Africa.

Kohv
in Estonian

LEGENDS OF COFFEE

The history of coffee is mostly shrouded in mystery and legend. The supposed origins of coffee are entertaining and varied, as most legends and tales tend to be—dubious in their verity, but generally regarded as the greatest and most romantic stories in history. Variations of the two most common, fanciful-but-unlikely stories go a little something like this…

Dancing Goats and Wandering Ghosts

One coffee legend regales us with the adventures of Omar, a dervish condemned by his enemies to wander and die of starvation in a desert outside the Arabic port of Mocha. (No, really, I'm not making this up.) Awakened at midnight by a ghostly apparition, the ravenous outcast recognizes it as the spirit of his dead mentor, who guides him to a coffee tree from which he picks the fruit and roasts its seeds. Omar tries to soften the beans in water and, when this fails, drinks the liquid. Instantly overcome by a physical sensation of well-being and newfound mental acuity, Omar makes his way back to Mocha to share his discovery. On the merit of simply having endured the rough desert conditions, Omar's survival is taken as a sign from God (as was everything else that could not be reasonably explained).

The other most widely quoted and favorite coffee legend of all time is about Kaldi, a young Ethiopian goatherd. He complains to the monks of a monastery in the southwestern province of Kaffa that he is regularly being kept up all night by his flock. According to Kaldi, the herd was "frisking and dancing in an unusual manner," prancing and cavorting on their hind legs after eating the fruit of certain berries. These days, we know what "frisking and dancing in an unusual manner" means, but back then the amorous nature of goats was perhaps not as fully understood as it is today. Back then, well, it was cause for alarm! And, of course, Mother Nature's urges

were not to blame—no! The sinister red berries were undoubtedly the cause of the goats' friskiness.

Encouraged by their frolicking, curious Kaldi tries the berries for himself. In some versions, a passing monk is astonished to see Kaldi and his flock merrily frisking and dancing together in a meadow (insert obvious bestiality joke here); while in others, a revved-up Kaldi simply shares his energy-producing findings with the monastery. After discovering the secret of Kaldi's newfound good nature, the monks begin using a caffeinated drink to keep awake during nightlong religious ceremonies. Today, Kaffa is known as the birthplace of coffee.

In some parts of Africa, coffee beans still are chewed. Raw beans soaked in water and spices are eaten like sweets. And just like their ancestors, some Ethiopians in parts of Kaffa and Sidamo—two of the world's main coffee-producing regions—still mix ground coffee beans with *nit'ir qibe,* a type of clarified butter similar to *ghee,* to give them a more luxurious flavour.

YEMEN: PLANTING THE SEED

Coffee should be black as Hell, strong as Death and sweet as love.

–Turkish proverb

A Miraculous Drink

For 300 years, coffee was drunk following the recipe first used by the Ethiopians. It wasn't until the 14th century that the Arabs discovered a new method for drinking coffee and began roasting the beans over a fire, then grinding them and boiling them in water.

Coffee came into general use in Islam in the middle of the 15th century, and the drink, first used in late-night religious ceremonies, began to take on a mythical status and started spreading throughout the Arab world.

According to one Persian legend, coffee was first served to a sleepy Muhammad by the angel Gabriel. In another story, King Solomon was said to have entered a town whose inhabitants were suffering from a mysterious ailment and, on Gabriel's command, he prepared a brew of roasted coffee beans and thereby cured the townspeople.

DID YOU KNOW?

Today, the word *kahwa* or *qahwa* is the Arabic word for coffee. Originally, however, *qahwa* was the Arabic word for wine. Since the Arabs didn't drink wine, coffee became known as the "wine of Islam."

Coffee Catches On

Increasingly, doctors began prescribing coffee to their ailing patients. At first only consumed on the advice of a physician or as part of a religious ceremony, coffee quickly became mainstream. Scholars, lawyers, artists and those who worked at night soon discovered the stimulating effects of coffee and eventually doctors no longer had to prescribe it and were drinking it themselves.

The first coffee houses were opened in Mecca around 1475 and were called *kaveh kanes*. They were lavish and extravagantly decorated, and sharing coffee quickly became ritual for people from all walks of life. Nothing quite like the coffee house had existed before—a place to meet, to relax or to conduct business in comfortable, good-smelling surroundings. Even more unusual, everyone was welcome and could enter for the price of a cup of coffee.

The Turks and Hindus believed that combining milk and coffee caused leprosy, so they always drank their coffee black.

Creating a Buzz

Khat (pronounced "cot") is a plant that contains a natural form of ephedrine. It originated in Ethiopia, where the natives chewed on the plant's young buds and fresh leaves. *Khat* was initially used socially to enhance excitation, banish sleep and promote communication. It was also used as a stimulant to dispel feelings of hunger and fatigue and, as you can imagine, was immensely popular. At first, the authorities in Yemen actively encouraged the newly introduced custom of coffee drinking as it was considered preferable to the extreme side effects of *khat*, which included inane laughing, delirium, euphoria and, in extreme cases, induced semi-comas. However, as coffee's popularity spread, that would quickly change.

Causing a Stir

As with all new things of this time, coffee was met with equal parts skepticism, enthusiasm and controversy. Because alcohol was forbidden, many Muslims embraced coffee as an alternative and were soon drinking it religiously. Unlike taverns, coffee houses were considered respectable gathering places. But they soon became hotspots of political activity, and some believed that coffee was intoxicating and should also be prohibited. Others feared its "magical" stimulating properties, and there were several attempts to ban coffee drinking over the next several decades. Luckily, they were always unsuccessful.

Coffee Prohibition

The earliest known attempt to ban the consumption of coffee occurred in June 1511, only months after the coffee houses had opened. Khair Beg, the governor of Mecca, banned coffee for fear that it would cause opposition to his rule. Coffee was seized and burned in the streets, and some vendors and customers were beaten as punishment for their iniquities. How badly would you want your next caffeine fix after that? Reportedly, some repeat offenders were sewn into leather bags and thrown into the nearest body of water.

Down But Not Out

Within a few months, though, the ban was overturned by the sultan, who declared coffee a sacred drink. Beg was executed, and the black liquid was soon flowing freely again.

Coffee may have been saved, but Muslim scholars still disapproved of the coffee houses—all they could see were hotbeds of gossip, rumor, political debate and satirical discussion. They were also popular venues for chess and backgammon, which, as everyone knows, are morally dubious games. It is said that the game of bridge originated in the coffee houses of Constantinople.

Technically, board games were only banned under Islamic law if bets were placed on their outcome. But the fact that they were played in the coffee houses gave another reason for critics to claim that such establishments were places of lax morality and dens for plotting, rebelling and rabble-rousing—no wonder people wanted to hang out there!

Further attempts to ban coffee in Mecca and Cairo were always short-lived and ultimately failed because no law was actually being broken by drinking coffee. Eventually, a solution was settled upon and coffee houses and coffee were taxed.

Coffee is the common man's gold, and like gold, it brings to every man the feeling of luxury and nobility.
–Sheik Abd-el-Kadir (1587)

TURKEY: BEAN EMBARGO

Fitting In

Accounts vary as to when and how coffee arrived in Turkey. Some say that it was Özdemir Pasha, the Ottoman governor of Yemen, who brought it as a gift to Sultan Suleiman in 1543; others say coffee was brought to Constantinople (now Istanbul) by two Syrian traders 10 years later in 1553.

Just as in Mecca, coffee quickly became a part of Turkish culture. The sultan would have his coffee prepared by highly skilled coffee makers known as *kahveci usta*. The chief coffee maker was chosen for his loyalty and his ability to keep secrets. Helped by sometimes as many as 40 assistants, coffee was served as part of an elaborate ceremony.

The first coffee house in Instanbul opened in 1554, and coffee soon became known as the "milk of chess players and thinkers." As an old Turkish proverb states, "The heart seeks neither coffee nor the coffee house. The heart seeks a friend; coffee is but an excuse."

Sea to Shining C

Mocha was the greatest port of its day and, because it was the main stop along the only sea route to Mecca, it was also the busiest port in the world at the time. But coffee was a jealously guarded commodity, and the Arabs did not want it being cultivated anywhere else. While Arab traders were keen to ship boiled or parched seeds the entire world over, they were careful never to allow beans that could germinate and create new coffee plants to leave Arabian borders. Since a coffee bean becomes infertile when stripped of its outer layer, live trees or beans had to be exported for a successful transplant. Thus, it was made illegal to export fertile beans.

Double Dutch

Of course, since exporting was made illegal, everyone started trying to smuggle it! The Dutch were the first to successfully smuggle live plants back to Holland in 1616, planting and carefully nurturing them in greenhouses. From there, they shipped them to faraway Dutch colonies, thereby bringing an end to the Arabian monopoly of the coffee trade. In 1696, the first colonial coffee estate was founded on Java, in Indonesia. Within a few years, the Dutch colonies had taken over as the main suppliers of coffee to Europe. Today, Indonesia is still the fourth largest exporter of coffee in the world. The Dutch were also responsible for bringing the plants to South America, which today is the coffee center of the world.

Coffee cherries imported from Yemen were sold in Egypt in the late 15th century as crystallized fruits and were considered great luxuries.

Brother Baba Budan and the Seven Seeds

Brother Baba Budan is the most widely credited with spreading coffee to India in 1670. His real name was Hazrat Shah Jamer Allah Mazarabi, but "Baba" stands for "papa." Baba Budan has been called everything from a revered holy man, a saint and a Muslim pilgrim to, well...a drug smuggler. In any case, the 17th-century Sufi went on a pilgrimage to Mecca and fell in love with the magic coffee beans. Since taking live coffee beans out of Mecca was punishable by death—more specifically, by beheading—Baba Budan had to be careful and managed to smuggle seven beans out of Arabia, wrapped around his belly. On his return to India, he planted the beans in the hills of Mysore, India, thereby bringing coffee to the East.

So yes, the caffeine that runs our lives was brought to us by the ingenuity of smugglers and drug dealers.

COFFEE POURS INTO EUROPE

Europeans learned about coffee more than 40 years before they had the opportunity to taste it. The first European to refer to coffee was a German physician and botanist named Leonhard Rauwolf, who traveled to the Middle East from 1573 to 1576. However, coffee didn't become widely available in Europe until around 1608, and even then, it was mostly for the upper class.

Venice, Italy

Venetian traders were introduced to coffee by Arabian merchants in 1615, who drank loads of the hot, bitter brew to fuel hours of bartering and bargaining. Coffee in Vienna was initially sold by lemonade vendors as an expensive medicinal beverage. Getting the same start in Venice as it had in Arabia, coffee was first available by prescription only.

The first coffee house in Venice didn't open until 1683, and the most famous of them all—Caffe Florian in Piazza San Marco—opened in 1720. Its doors are still open for business today. By 1763, there were well over 2000 coffee shops in the city.

Sobering Thoughts

Quick—what was the most common thing to drink at breakfast in the 1600s? Well, let's see—there's orange juice, water, coffee or tea? Well actually, it was none of the above. It was beer, of course! Or wine. You might either think this sounds terrible, or that it's a really great idea. The truth is that both were far safer to drink than the water, which was filthy and contaminated. If that isn't a great excuse for consuming alcohol daily, then I don't know what is! It was even considered perfectly normal for children to drink alcohol, and the average European at this time consumed around six pints of beer every day. Until coffee came along in the mid-1600s, most of Europe had been mildly intoxicated for centuries.

Think about it—it would have been like an entire society of Homer Simpsons. It didn't even occur to anyone that they might function better without it (drunken logic, probably). Even Queen Elizabeth I knocked back a few each morning with her meat stew. Given this habitual bender, Europeans generally muddled through their daily existence in the grip of an alcoholic haze. Drunkenness was standard and, well, wasn't even called drunkenness; it was a normal state of being. So it's no wonder that coffee was embraced with such fervor and delight. Suddenly, there was something that alerted the mind rather than numbed it.

Enlightenment by the Cup

For the first time in history, humans could manage their sleep hours, began developing a routine and started keeping a regular work schedule. Coffee's epic arrival onto the scene shook Europe out of its lethargic fog, getting people to think more clearly and helping them get things done. What a triumph! It wasn't called the "Age of Reason" for nothing. Maybe it should have been called the "Detox Decade" or, better yet, "Sobering Up: The Early Years."

Cup of Old Shoe, Anyone?

The coffee of the 17th century must have tasted terrible. Because it was taxed by the gallon, coffee had to be brewed in advance. Cold coffee from the barrel was then re-boiled before serving. It has been described as tasting like "syrup of soot" or the "essence of old shoes." All the same, this still didn't seem to dissuade most people from drinking it.

Many members of the clergy encouraged coffee guzzling because they wanted parishioners to stay awake during their sermons.

An Excellent Way to Prevent and Cure "the Dropsy"

Coffee was most commonly prescribed as a diuretic. Known as a "tonic brew," it was also believed to cure everything from colds, headaches, rheumatism, consumption, scurvy, gout, kidney stones, the dropsy, eye sores and, of course, miscarriages.

From Sinner to Saint

Believe it or not, we have the pope to thank for the proliferation of our morning java guzzling. Christian priests believed that

Satan had invented coffee as a substitute for wine, which Muslims did not drink. Fearing the power of "the devil's cup," legend goes that Vatican officials asked the Pope to impose a ban on the Satanic brew. Pope Clement VIII refused to do so before tasting it for himself. In 1605, a steaming cup was brought before him and, like most of the world, Clement was immediately "enchanted." Not only did he not condemn it, he enjoyed the taste and aroma so much that he baptized it, so that all Christians could drink the beverage without guilt or prescription. He is reported to have said, "Why, this Satan's drink is so delicious that it would be a pity to let the infidels have exclusive use of it. We shall cheat Satan by baptizing it." Critics were dismayed. The Pope's endorsement removed coffee's biggest potential obstacle and massive quantities of the good stuff were soon imported to Italy and the rest of the Western world.

Turkish Delight

Suleiman Aga, the Turkish ambassador, arrived in Paris in 1669 with coffee beans and an important message from his sultan to the King of France. Louis XIV, a notorious egomaniac, was offended at Aga's peasant garb and, after receiving the sultan's letter, told the ambassador that he'd get around to reading it when he felt like it, which ended up being about a year.

Having no choice but to wait around, Aga made the most of his time in Paris by renting a palace that can only be described as "over the top." Being the good Turk that he was, Aga began hosting elaborate coffee parties, whipping the *femmes* of Paris into a frenzy with his thick, black Turkish coffee. And, oh, what a charmer he was! The Parisians literally ate it up and drank it in. His guests—mostly women—were mesmerized by the exotic surroundings, the plush cushions, the black slaves and the remarkable coffee.

This sparked what can only be described as Turkomania, or Turkeypolooza; it was a veritable Turkoganza! This new and exotic ritual filtered into every upper class salon in Paris, though it's laughable to picture dainty 17th-century Frenchwomen sporting turbans and ornamental robes, taking their coffee *à la Turque*. These parties are described by Isaac D'Israeli in his *Curiosities of Literature:*

> *On bended knee, the black slaves of the Ambassador, arrayed in the most gorgeous Oriental costumes, served the choicest*

Mocha coffee in tiny cups of egg-shell porcelain, hot, strong and fragrant, poured out in saucers of Gold and silver, placed on embroidered silk doylies fringed with gold bullion, to the grand dames, who fluttered their fans with many grimaces, bending their piquant faces—be-rouged, be-powdered and be-patched—over the new and steaming beverage.

Loose Lips Sink Ships...and Lead to Invasion

But Louis XIV wasn't paying much attention to the Turkish messenger. He had a bankrupt country to worry about, three mistresses and the gout. So Suleiman Aga managed to be very successful with his secret mission. Having nothing else to do but sit around, drink coffee and gossip, Aga managed to get plenty of information from the Parisian aristocrats, who were not known for their discretion.

In reality, the sultan had a secret plan to invade Vienna and had sent Aga to find out if he had an ally in Louis XIV. He didn't, but that information was never shared with the king; it came from the same lips that were indulging in the rich Turkish coffee—lips loosened by caffeine and comfortable seating.

When ambassador Aga returned to Istanbul, his coffee brewer stayed in France and opened a coffee house to serve Turkish coffee.

Molière Digs In

Even playwrights got in on the fun. In 1670, Molière wrote a satire called *Le Bourgeois Gentilhomme*, which poked fun at the pretentious middle class and the vain, arrogant aristocracy. The title, which translates to "bourgeois gentleman," is an oxymoron, since Molière believed that there was no such thing. The play reflected the then-current trend for *les turqueries* and stemmed from the scandal caused by Suleiman Aga when he pulled one over on the king and his court.

In Europe, the most obstreperous nations are those most addicted to coffee. We rightly speak of a "storm in a teacup" as the tiniest disturbance in the world, but out of a coffee-cup comes hurricanes.
–Robert Wilson Lynd, Irish author and essayist

To the Victor Go the Spoils

It was the Turks who brought coffee to Austria when their army surrounded Vienna in 1683, laying siege to the city. After attacking Vienna for two months, the Turkish army was finally driven back by an army of about 50,000 mainly Polish soldiers.

Franz George Kolschitzky is most commonly credited with leading the victory. Having spent time in Turkey as an interpreter, Kolschitzky proved to be an excellent spy because he was able to pass himself off as a Turkish soldier. He ran information between the Viennese and the Polish army, and the story goes that it was Kolschitzy's spy work that led relief forces to the city.

Camel Food

It is said that the retreating Turks left not only their hope of conquering Europe behind, but guns, gold, oxen, camels and bags and bags of green coffee beans. The swag was divvied up among the victorious troops, but there were no takers for the green beans, which everyone mistook for camel food. One story reports that the coffee beans were dumped into the Danube.

In a fortuitous turn of events, another rendition of the story tells how Kolschitzky just happened to be the only one who recognized the value of the beans. He took the beans and went door to door, serving coffee to all the parched citizens before setting up shop in a large tent open to the public. He eventually opening a coffee house called The Blue Bottle in a building he had been given for his wartime efforts.

In truth, it is much more likely that Kolschitzky did not single-handedly bring defeat to the Turks. Many historians believe that there were actually half a dozen spies involved in the war effort. The first Viennese café was actually opened in 1685 by an Armenian named Johannes Diodato. Some say that Kolschitzky was a fraud and a cheat; others consider him a hero and important part of Viennese history.

However, it is believed that the Viennese—which may or may not have included Kolschitzky—*did* introduce the idea of filtering coffee, as well as sweetening it with milk and sugar. Before that, the brew was strong and black, and the Turks left the grounds in the bottom of the cup after pressing them.

Although it is all conjecture, some also credit Kolschitzky with introducing coffee to its inseparable better half—the pastry. Wanting to commemorate his contribution to the war effort, one Viennese baker began making rolls shaped like the crescent on the Turkish flag, and thus the croissant was born. Everyone loves a good story, especially when both pastries and bravery are involved.

The Turkish word for breakfast, *kahvalti*, literally means "before coffee."

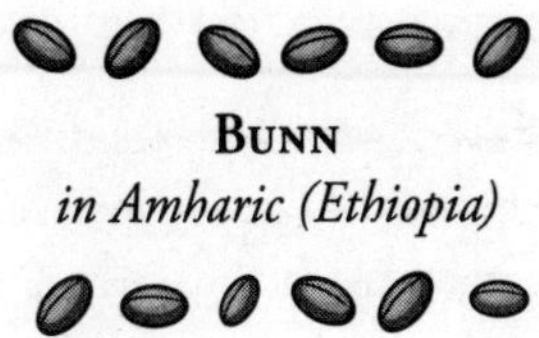

THE LONDON COFFEE HOUSE: THE STARBUCKS OF THE 17TH CENTURY

Think that Starbucks was the first coffee company ever to be ubiquitous? Truth is that coffee shops in Constantinople and Damascus were the prototypes of the great Western coffee houses—and Starbucks ain't got nothin' on the coffee houses of 17th-century London. The first coffee house opened in Britain in the 1650s and in Amsterdam during the 1660s, spreading west until all of Europe was buzzing. During this time, Londoners drank more coffee than any other citizens in the world, though Constantinople would have been a close second. Considering that neither of these cities is renowned for their coffee-drinking today, it shows how central to social, commercial and political life the coffee houses became. Before the Internet and Facebook, there was the coffee house, the original social network.

England (1650–1775)

Puritan Oliver Cromwell, also known as Old Ironsides, came to power at the end of the English civil war after King Charles I was dethroned and executed in 1649.

It is widely believed that Puritans were strict, hard-nosed suppressors of creativity who ruled England with an iron fist. The Puritans are historically known to have been real killjoys—they banned Christmas, closed the theaters, prohibited sports on Sundays, made "tippling" (drinking excessively) illegal and outlawed swearing. They believed that pointless, "frivolous" enjoyment served no purpose. *Boo!*

But surprisingly, they were also responsible for women's sexual liberation, improved overall personal hygiene and granted freedom of the press. See, they weren't all bad—and to boot, the Puritans played a large part in the evolution of the coffee house.

The Golden Age of the Coffee House

Not surprisingly, following Cromwell's death in 1658, most of Britain began second-guessing its decision to become a republic; suddenly, the monarchy didn't seem so bad after all! After Cromwell's restrictive reign, men were thirsting for more than just coffee—they needed centers for social gathering where they could discuss the daily events and the world's happenings. The people were seeking freedom.

And coffee houses were the perfect forum. They became centers of political debate, which opened the door for Charles II to become king in 1660. It is generally believed that the king might not have gained his throne were it not for the frequent gathering of his supporters and the liberty of speech provided in the coffee houses. The coffee house was to become pulpit, courtroom, stage and classroom. By 1700, there were even coffee houses in Russia, which was known primarily as being a tea-drinking nation.

Coffee was usually drunk black and unsweetened in London coffee houses, but some customers added cinnamon, cloves, spearmint, molasses, sugar, sour cream, butter, oatmeal, mustard or, of course, ale.

Beer Wins Out in Germany

One of the few places where coffee wasn't trumping alcohol as the most popular beverage was in Germany, which is still known today for its enthusiastic consumption of beer. It was one of the last European countries to see the appearance of coffee houses, with an establishment finally opening in Berlin in 1721. Why?

It was considered unmanly to drink coffee, which to them might as well have been a fruity slush drink served with an umbrella. Afternoon coffee became a standard occasion for women, and the men even coined the derogatory term *Kaffeeklatsch* to refer to women's gossip at these events. Today, *Kaffeeklatsch* has become a broader term meaning relaxed conversation in general, similar to what we would call "chitchat" in English.

Even though it was only the women who gathered over cups of coffee, it was generally believed that drinking coffee could make a woman sterile; instead, women were advised (probably by the men) to drink more beer.

The bustling city of Hamburg was the center of the pickled herring industry—the thirst created by the salty fish was better quenched with beer than with coffee. This really explains quite a lot.

The Coffee Police

Just as in Mecca before, coffee was once again at the center of controversy. It seems there was always someone complaining about coffee.

In 1775, Frederick the Great banned coffee in Prussia, saying, "My people must drink beer." Let's just let that sit for a while. While for most, that declaration may seem like a gift from the heavens, but for the good coffee-drinking citizens of Prussia, it was cause for outrage. The story goes that Frederick did not believe that coffee-drinking soldiers could be relied upon, but in truth, it was an attempt to bolster flagging beer sales and to try to stimulate the nation's economy. He did more than just ban it, though—he stepped it up a notch. Under his orders, the government hired a special force called—are you ready for this?—the *Kaffee Schnüfflers*, or "coffee sniffers," to *schnüff* out any illicit coffee roasters and smugglers.

Public outcry did, however, cause the king to rescind the policy, especially since the nobility, the clergy and all the high officials were still allowed to drink coffee. Rumor had it that the king

himself loved coffee as much as his people, so when a revolt broke out—as with every other ban in the history of coffee—it didn't last very long.

In 1732, Johann Sebastian Bach composed an entire cantata poking fun at those who opposed coffee on medical "grounds." Some argued that women who drank coffee could not bear children; others claimed that it "burned up the blood, induced palsies, impotence and leanness." The *Kaffeekantate* satirized the annoyance of German women against the ridiculous restrictions surrounding its use.

Men Against Women

Coffee leads men to trifle away their time, scald their chops, and spend their money, all for a little base, black, thick, nasty, bitter, stinking nauseous puddle water.

–The Women's Petition Against Coffee (1674)

In 1674, English women became increasingly upset at all the time their menfolk were spending at the coffee houses—it was like competing for time with a mistress! They joined forces to create "The Women's Petition Against Coffee," claiming that coffee was a heathen that had made their men as "unfruitful as the deserts where that unhappy berry is said to be bought." The men, undeterred by the petition, penned their own equally vivid retort:

You may well permit us to talk abroad, for at home, we have scarce time to utter a word for the insufferable Din of your ever active Tongues, the Foolish extravagancies of our lives, are infinitly out-done by the wild Frolliques of yours; the truth is, Coffee rather assists us for your Nocturnal Benevolences, by drying up those Crude Flatulent Humours, which otherwise would make us only Flash in the Pan.

I Get Knocked Down, But I Get Back Up Again

Tavern keepers, of course, were also unhappy that their liquor profits were spilling over to the coffee houses, but all of the objections were of no use. By 1663, there were 83 coffee houses in London. Many of them were destroyed in the Great Fire of 1666, but even more were built in their place.

Some Things Never Change

Knowing firsthand the influence and power wielded by the coffee house, Charles II tried to close them down on December 29, 1675. Their tendency to be a breeding ground for hatching political plots is exactly what had helped him get back into power, but now it concerned him.

He denounced the coffee houses as "dangerous and evil establishments" and rescinded their licenses, allowing them only two weeks to close. Coffee houses, though, had already become so integrated into the fabric of London society that the king was forced to withdraw the order 11 days later after overwhelming public outcry. It quickly became clear that the king's proclamation was going to be soundly ignored, which would have undermined the government's authority.

Home and Away

Attempts to control coffee imports only led to increased smuggling. By 1688, coffee also began making an appearance at breakfast and dinner in the homes of the upper class. By 1714, there were over 2000 coffee houses in London, catering to every class of society. Each art and profession had their own hangout; doctors, lawyers, booksellers, authors, playwrights, businessmen, politicians and artists all had a home away from home. In fact, British poet, historian and politician Thomas Macaulay actually described the coffee house as the "Londoner's home," and those who wished to find a gentleman asked not where his residence was but which coffee house he frequented.

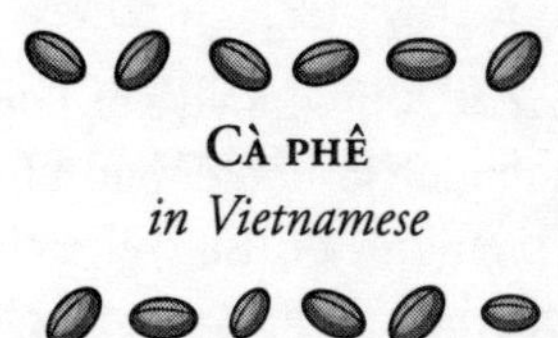

FROM COFFEE RAGS TO RICHES

The Shipping News

In 1688, Edward Lloyd opened a coffee house in London. It was initially a gathering place solely for sailors, ship owners and merchants. Next door to the post office, Lloyd had easy access to shipping lists and started preparing the maritime news for his clients. Shortly after opening, members of the shipping industry started to visit Lloyd's shop to discuss insurance with each other. Maritime insurance brokers soon found it easier to search for subscribers in coffee houses instead of trailing them from office to office.

Get a Leg Up

Today, Lloyd's of London is one of the largest insurance markets in the world. Lloyd's is known for insuring unusual and specialty items and have insured everything from food critic Egon Ronay's taste buds to guitarist Keith Richards' hands to rocker Bruce Springsteen's voice. They are best known for insuring the legs of famous people such as *Lord of the Dance* Michael Flatley, dancer Fred Astaire, soccer star David Beckham, actress Betty Grable, singer Tina Turner and model Heidi Klum.

Taste Sensation

Most recently, in March 2009, Lloyd's of London insured an Italian coffee taster's tongue for more than £10 million. Gennaro Pelliccia works for a premium British coffee chain and personally tastes and grades more than 5000 types of coffee each year. After 18 years of tasting, it is said that Pelliccia's tongue is the most expensive in the business, securing itself a place in the *Guinness World Records*. He claims to be able to distinguish thousands of different flavors and identify faults and defective qualities in each type of coffee. But having such a talented tongue is not

without its sacrifices—Pelliccia has to be careful not to burn his tongue or eat food that is too spicy lest it dull his lingual sensitivity.

Quick Shot

 Coffee houses are credited with being the birthplace of the stock exchange, as stockbrokers often frequented Garraway's coffee house. In today's London Stock Exchange, the attendants are still called waiters.

 The Turk's Head coffee house introduced the ballot box. Referred to as the "wooden oracle," it was first used when

particularly heated discussions could only be settled by casting votes.

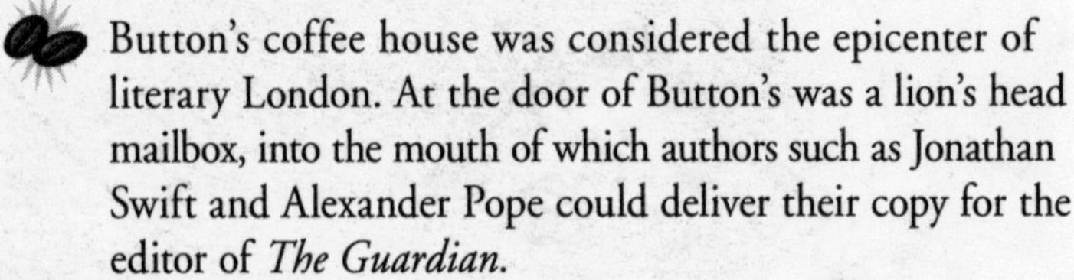

- Button's coffee house was considered the epicenter of literary London. At the door of Button's was a lion's head mailbox, into the mouth of which authors such as Jonathan Swift and Alexander Pope could deliver their copy for the editor of *The Guardian.*

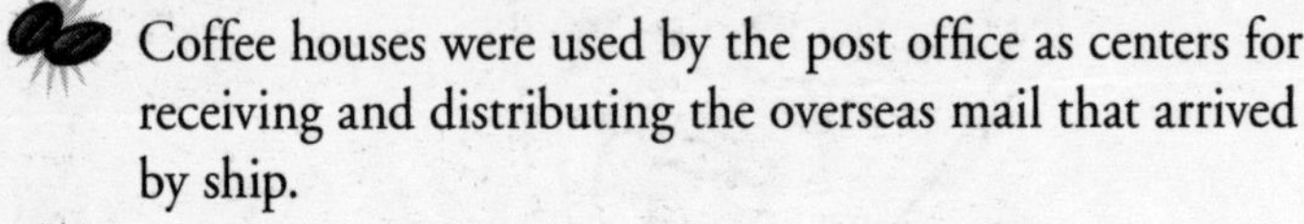

- Coffee houses were used by the post office as centers for receiving and distributing the overseas mail that arrived by ship.
- Apart from the serving wenches, women were not allowed in the coffee houses.
- Alexander Pope's poem "The Rape of the Lock" developed from coffee house gossip.

Penny Universities

Coffee houses were open to the general public for one penny. As long as patrons were willing to abide by the rules, everyone could listen in on the repartee of writers, politicians, artists, bankers and even adventurers. For this reason, coffee houses became known as "penny universities." Part of their vast appeal was that they were full of otherwise-ordinary famous people who had opinions about everything. Inside the coffee houses, new trends were blazed and good taste in art and literature was developed. Liberty of speech was utmost, and knowledge and information was shared like never before. On the other hand, as you might expect, so was scandal and gossip, and many reputations were made or broken over a cup of coffee.

Here's a Tip

A common misconception about the gratuity known as the "tip" is that early coffee houses used to place a box marked "T.I.P." in a prominent location as a suggestion to customers to ante up a little

extra money "to insure promptness" in service. However, the word "insure" does not mean the same thing as its homonym "ensure," which is the proper spelling to use in this case, leaving us with a gratuity known as the "tep." The true origin of the word "tip" is thought to be in the 1700s among gamblers and thieves who used the word to refer to giving or sharing their winnings and wealth.

The Original National Enquirer

Some may be surprised to learn that that London's original gossip rag was actually started by a man. *The Tatler* and *The Spectator* both got their start in coffee houses, since there was no better place to gather information, or readers. Originally meant to be newspapers that dealt with politics and news, the publishers quickly learned that fashion, entertainment and good old-fashioned gossip were of much more interest to their readers, and therefore much more profitable. *The Tatler* covered current affairs and important issues of the day such as duels, gambling and discussions on good manners. *The Spectator* focused mainly on literary criticism, cultural and moral issues. Both newspapers had a huge impact on etiquette and good taste, and considered themselves the "voices of a new and civilized urban life."

DECLINE OF THE GOLDEN ERA

Over time, however, the English coffee houses slowly began to decline. The establishments loosened their entrance rules and started serving alcohol. Vagabonds seeking refuge and undesirables looking to profit from rich travelers were allowed onto the premises. The establishments lost their friendly atmosphere, became more dangerous and were increasingly abandoned. The literati formed their own literary and political clubs, and the businessmen migrated back to their offices. By the end of the 18th century, the coffee house cup was all but empty.

Tea Takes Over

Tea quickly became the new kid on the block and was first served to the public in England in Garraway's coffee house around 1657. Catherine of Braganza, who married Charles II in 1662, brought the Portuguese custom of drinking tea to the English court. Tea began gaining social status as ladies in their drawing rooms encouraged tea drinking, a fad that grew so rapidly the government did what all governments do when faced with semi-popular goods—they taxed it.

The British East India Company Stakes Its Claim

Initially created by a group of local businessmen in London who banded together simply to make money importing spices, the British East India Company ended up forging a formidable monopoly, assembling its own military and administrative departments and more or less becoming an imperial power unto itself. It is said to have been "a Company that Owned a Nation."

The British East India Company, profiting from increased imports from the Far East, did everything possible to encourage the consumption of tea. Tea had a number of good things going for it—no one could deny that it was easier to prepare at home than its high-maintenance cousin, requiring only boiling water instead of roasting, grinding and brewing. It was also easier and quicker to transport tea from India than it was to bring in coffee from Asia and Africa—this meant it was cheaper and more readily available. Between 1700 and 1757, average annual tea imports into England more than quadrupled to about £4 million, and consumption continued to grow steadily. And so it was that England became a nation of tea drinkers, leaving the coffee houses to become a symbol of a bygone Golden Era.

If this is coffee, please bring me some tea; but if this is tea, please bring me some coffee.

–Abraham Lincoln

The Boston Tea Party

But just as the British were taking their last sips of coffee, the Americans were beginning to lift cup to lips.

It was the British tax on tea that led to the Boston Tea Party. The tax essentially shut out American tea merchants and granted preferential treatment to the British East India Company. Angered by the move, a group of about 50 Americans threw 342 chests of British tea into Boston Harbor on December 16, 1773. The boycott, of course, was planned in a coffee house.

The Boston Tea Party led to a general boycott of British goods and sparked the American War of Independence in 1775. At the time, tea was actually the preferred drink of Americans, but it was quickly considered more patriotic to refuse to drink tea, and coffee soon became a symbol of American Independence. Since that time, Americans have primarily been coffee drinkers.

And quit bringing up our forefathers and saying they were Civil Libertarians…they were blowing people's heads off because they put a tax on their breakfast beverage—and it wasn't even coffee.

–Dennis Miller

The Spread of the Coffee House

1511	Mecca	1683	Venice
1532	Cairo	1685	Vienna
1554	Constantinople	1694	Leipzig
1652	London	1696	New York
1655	Oxford	1700	Salzburg
1664	Cambridge	1703	Philadelphia
1670	Boston	1714	Prague
1671	Paris	1718	Stockholm
1673	Edinburgh	1721	Berlin
1673	Glasgow	Late 18th c.	Madrid
1673	Bremen		

PARIS COFFEE HOUSES

The cafés of Paris outlasted the British coffee houses since they managed to evolve with the times. Not only had they had always served wine and liquor, which created stability and helped them last longer, but many also served excellent food and became fine restaurants. And come on, no one is better at doing nothing, wasting time and complaining than the French. Today, coffee is said to be the "fuel of France."

The City that Never Sleeps

Many of the French cafés of the late 1600s were in the less fashionable parts of the city, so it was considered quite daring to be a coffee drinker. And because of its links to both the American and, later, French Revolutions, coffee was considered to be a "subversive" beverage. By 1690, Paris had over 300 cafés and, by 1840,

there were well over 3000. Paris was described as being centered around one vast, continuous coffee house that never slept.

Coffee and coffee houses seem too much an expression of the French sensibility to ever disappear easily, since behind every Parisian there is a waiter, a revolutionary and a gourmand.

–Schapira brothers, authors of *The Book of Coffee & Tea*

Dutch Treat

Not only were the Dutch instrumental in spreading coffee to their colonies all over the world, but to Europe as well. In 1714, the French received a coffee plant as a gift from the mayor of Amsterdam. In fact, the coffee trees planted in the garden at Versailles were direct descendants of the plants smuggled out of Mocha by the Dutch a century earlier. Coffee remained a drink affordable only to the rich in the time of Louis XIV, and it is widely believed that the tradition of adding sugar to coffee began in his court. Some also estimate that eventually 90 percent of the world's coffee would come from the seeds of this one plant.

Royal Flush

The next time you complain about your job, think of the chair-bearers of the 16th century. Introduced during the reign of François I (1515–47), chair-bearers carried around His Majesty's portable toilet and attended to his "royal needs." This was actually considered to be a very prestigious career choice since it meant getting to spend "intimate time" with the king.

Toilet Armchairs

But it was really Louis XIV and Louis XV who were known for their toilet armchairs. Louis XIV announced his marriage to Madame de Maintenon while on his *chaise d'affaires* ("business seat"). And Louis XV left nearly 300 toilet seats behind at the

Palace of Versailles, according to an inventory conducted shortly before the French Revolution.

And what does this have to do with coffee? Well, Louis XIV was known for having a "delicate stomach." In other words, he was frequently constipated. So coffee, which was known as a digestive aid and diuretic, would help pass the time, among other things. And the toilet armchair would ensure that no opportunity passed by unexploited.

The Coffee King

It wasn't until the days of his successor Louis XV that coffee was really injected into the societal bloodstream.

Louis XV loved coffee, though his love for it may have had more to do with impressing his mistress than with the drink itself. The Royal Gardens housed about 10 coffee trees, which

would produce roughly six pounds of beans annually. The king himself would personally harvest, roast and brew coffee for himself and his special friends. He spent lavishly, and his coffee-roasting soirées with his royal mistress, Madame du Barry, were something of a scandal.

He reportedly spent the equivalent of $15,000 a year to feed his daughter's coffee habit in the late 1600s. By 1740, the price had dropped to around 50 cents a cup, making coffee much more affordable for the common folk.

DID YOU KNOW?

In 1710, instead of boiling it, the French poured hot water through grounds in cloth bag. This is referred to as infusion brewing, a method of brewing that came to be known as the "French press."

Café Procope

In 1686, the most famous café in all of Europe was opened by an Italian named Francesco Procopio dei Coltelli. The café was across the street from the new Comédie Française, a famous French royal theater, and soon became the natural gathering place of actors, writers, musicians, dramatists and poets. This marked the beginning of some serious coffee drinking in Paris.

The list of idea-pondering, plot-hatching, coup-planning free-thinkers that frequented the establishment is impressive to say the least: Victor Hugo, Jean-Jacques Rousseau, Honoré de Balzac, George Sand, Jean de La Fontaine, Paul Verlaine and Voltaire all drank their way through two centuries worth of coffee at Café Procope. It is also rumored that Marat, Danton and Robespierre plotted the French Revolution there, and a poor artillery officer by the name of Napoleon Bonaparte often stopped in to play chess and usually had to surrender his tricornered hat as collateral for his unpaid coffee—or so the story goes. Sarah Bernhardt, a French stage actress, relaxed between her roles in the Café Procope, and Denis Diderot worked on his *Encyclopédie* there, supported by his wife, who would give him nine *sous* every day to buy his coffee.

Today, Café Procope is considered "the Holy Grail" of Parisien cafés. Its caffeine-fuelled exchange of information established a grand legacy of coffee-house culture, even today.

Popular Americans in France

Benjamin Franklin visited France in 1776 and was so enormously popular that he won French military support for the rebel American colonists. Of course, he visited Café Procope, as did Thomas Jefferson, and impressed the coffee-drinking leaders of the French Revolution so much that when he died in 1790, the café walls were draped in black as a sign of respect.

Coffee should be black as the devil, hot as hell, pure as an angel and as sweet as love.
–Charles Maurice de Talleyrand Périgord (1754–1838), French statesman

Revolution At The Bottom Of Their Cups

In July 1789, it was in the coffee houses around the Palais Royal where a young journalist by the name of Camille Desmoulins jumped up on a table and began a fiery speech that moved the caffeinated throngs to march off immediately, overcome with revolutionary fervor. Two days later, the Bastille fell.

WRITERS AND THEIR COFFEE

I don't get people who don't like coffee, and I distrust writers who don't drink it. How can anyone be a writer without coffee? Writers are the original Coffee Achievers.

–Joseph Finder, author

Fuelling Creativity

Here are a few examples of why writing and coffee go hand in hand:

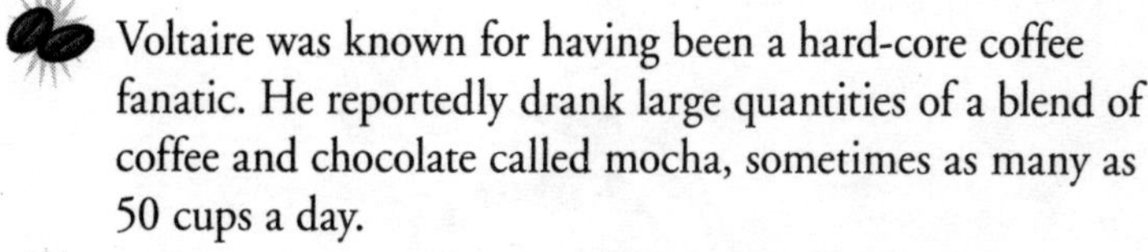

- Voltaire was known for having been a hard-core coffee fanatic. He reportedly drank large quantities of a blend of coffee and chocolate called mocha, sometimes as many as 50 cups a day.
- Jean-Jacques Rousseau, a French philosopher who wrote about education and politics, was known to admire the smell of freshly roasted coffee, penning: "Ah, that is a perfume in which I delight; when they roast coffee near my house, I hasten to open the door to take in all the aroma."
- Sir Arthur Conan Doyle, along with his fictional sleuth Sherlock Holmes, both loved coffee almost as much as they loved cocaine.
- Edgar Allen Poe drank coffee by the gallon, which begs the question: was the beating of the *Tell-Tale Heart* a matter of conscience or just the effects of a caffeine overdose?
- Hemingway wrote his famous novel *A Farewell to Arms* at a railway café in Montreux, Switzerland.

If Balzac Lived Today, He'd Have Been a Truck Driver

When we drink coffee, ideas march in like the army.

–Honoré de Balzac

If there had ever been a coffee-lovers contest, the great Honoré de Balzac would have been the winner. He was a hard-core coffee fanatic, a real man's man. He had thick black hair, big square hands and legs shaped like bowling pins. He was also your typical tortured French writer—he wrote 16 hours a day and loved his coffee as much as his women, his opium and his dinner.

Balzac used to eat his coffee. Yep, that's right. He chewed right on the beans. Think he used to take his coffee with a side of crazy? Well, the thing about coffee is that its stimulating effects only really last two or three weeks before the body gets used to it. Balzac drank so much coffee that eating it was the only way to overcome his caffeine tolerance. All he had to do was dump the raw grounds into an empty stomach.

"Coffee roasts your insides," he wrote in his essay "The Pleasures and Pains of Coffee," and rightly so. Not for the faint of heart, raw coffee will essentially eat away at your stomach lining, acting like a potent jet fuel and propelling the eater to think and remember things like never before. Don't try this at home, though, because it will also kill you.

Coffee killed Balzac in the end. Not surprisingly, he suffered from intense stomach cramps, high blood pressure and an enlarged heart. Ulcers completely ate through his stomach, and he died from a combination of that and acute caffeine poisoning.

But at least no one can ever accuse him of being a wimp.

> *The best maxim I know in life is to drink your coffee when you can, and when you cannot, be easy without it.*
> –Jonathan Swift (1667–1745), Irish satirist and poet

Enema at the Gates

But not everyone loved coffee. It is said that the Duchess of Orleans, Louis XIV's German sister-in-law, compared it to the Archbishop of Paris's breath. Madame de Sévigné, a French aristocrat famous for her letters, was also unimpressed. In a letter to her daughter, she said: "There are two things Frenchmen will never swallow—the poetry of Racine, and coffee." Oscar Wilde complained that the French never learned to make a cup of coffee that did not taste like a mouthful of swamp mud. Another French nobleman used coffee solely as an enema and remarked that it did the job very well.

NO SUBSTITUTE FOR COFFEE

Mind-Boggling Concoctions

The typical reasons for additives in coffee are economic. When Frederick the Great of Prussia put coffee under an expensive state monopoly in 1781, the poorer classes tried a myriad of strange and unsuccessful substitutes for the real thing, including barley, wheat, corn, chicory and dried figs, each roasted and ground.

In England, after the Great Fire of 1666, the British tried even more alarming alternatives, such as betony—the root of a plant belonging to the mint family—and "bocket" or "saloop," a veritable witches' brew made by extracting sap from the sassafras tree, then combining it with sugar and boiling it. Needless to say, once the shortage was over, coffee came pouring back in a hurry.

The list of possible substitutes is endless. All types of grains, acorns, sugar cane, molasses and even pieces of bread—roasted and ground—have been tried as coffee substitutes. An impressive variety of nuts, cereals and vegetables have been used, proving that there is no end to the lengths people will go for caffeine. Acorns, beans, beetroots, carrots, juniper berries, rice—you name it, it's probably been made into coffee at one time or another.

When coffee supplies became scarce during the American Civil War, soldiers desperate for a cup of coffee roasted sweet potatoes, Indian corn and the seed of the okra plant as coffee substitutes.

"Successful" Substitutes

Dandelion root is still used today as a coffee substitute and can be bought pre-ground or in soluble form from health food stores.

It closely resembles coffee in flavor and body and, when brewed properly, is reportedly quite delicious.

Another substitute that is somewhat popular is dried or roasted figs. The combination, made popular in Vienna, is now mass-produced and known as Viennese coffee.

Chicory Root

The use of chicory originated in Holland in 1770, and it has been used as a coffee substitute in Europe ever since. In 1806, Napoleon declared France self-sufficient and promoted chicory over coffee. The roots are also used as a coffee additive, especially in the Mediterranean region where the plant is native. It is also popular in India and parts of Southeast Asia. Chicory is used as a sweetener in the food industry, as it has a sweetening power stronger than that of sucrose. Today, it is still used as a cheap coffee substitute in U.S. prisons.

The island of St. Helena, still a British protectorate, lies in the Atlantic Ocean, 1200 miles (2000 kilometers) from Africa and 2200 miles (3500 kilometers) from Brazil. It is best known for being the island to which Napoléon Bonaparte was exiled in 1815 after the battle of Waterloo. He died there in 1821 and is reported to have said that the only good thing to come from this tiny island was its coffee.

Kope

in Hawaiian

COFFEE IN NORTH, SOUTH AND CENTRAL AMERICA

American Coffee Houses

Captain John Smith is generally credited for introducing coffee to the New World in 1607 in Jamestown, Virginia. Canadian historians suggest it may have previously been introduced in Canada. Either way, coffee could never have been grown in such cold climates.

As Always, Women Do All the Work

It was women who opened the first coffee houses in America. Coffee houses were not quite as popular as they had been in Europe because American settlers were primarily Puritans and felt that prayer and hard work were the most important habits to cultivate. Hours spent in a public house were considered sinful, so those in power gave the first license to sell coffee to a woman, Dorothy Jones of Boston, in 1670. It was thought that, as a woman, she would be on "better terms with the Devil." Although women operated coffee houses and served in them, just as in Europe, they were still not allowed to frequent the coffee houses as patrons.

Around 1668, New Yorkers began substituting coffee for beer at breakfast—shortly afterwards, the New York coffee houses began to flourish. Rather than influencing the arts like their European counterparts, the New York cafés contained long assembly rooms where court trial and council meetings could be held.

The Tontine coffee house served as the New York Stock Exchange after it was built in 1791. It was described as an elaborate and pretentious building and became a great tourist attraction. Great balls and banquets were held here, and no trip to New York was considered complete without a visit to the Tontine.

A Swashbuckling Story

In 1723, three coffee plants arrived in Martinique, a French colony. How they got there is another one of coffee's great yarns. A young naval officer, Gabriel Mathieu de Clieu, is most commonly given credit for having tenaciously smuggled the trees to Martinique after his formal request was denied by the king. On leave from Martinique and unwilling to take "no" for an answer, the story paints de Clieu as being single-handedly responsible for the spread of the coffee plant to the Caribbean.

Several versions of the tale have de Clieu leading a moonlight raid, scaling castle walls and breaking into the Royal Gardens to steal a sprout of the precious coffee plant; others have him convincing the gardener's mistress to sweet-talk her lover into giving her a sprig for de Clieu.

The Coffee Plant Gets a Secret Service Agent

De Clieu set sail for Martinique, carefully protecting the coffee plant in a glass case on deck so that it received adequate heat and sunlight, and to protect it from the damaging salt water. And here the story gets really whimsical—en route, not only do Tunisian pirates raid the ship, but a violent storm puts the precious plant in danger! Then, if that wasn't enough, an enemy on board tries to sabotage the plant and a violent struggle ensues wherein a branch is torn off, but luckily is kept alive and intact. And lastly, near the end of the journey, a lack of fresh water forces de Clieu to make the ultimate sacrifice for his country—he gives up half of his daily water ration to the plant to ensure that it survives until they reach the shores of Martinique. De Clieu—a true hero for all mankind.

A Legend in His Own Mind

As it turns out, the origin of this story is straight from de Clieu himself—from his personal journals—and there is no corroborating evidence that this account was anything more than a fanciful, albeit imaginative, fabrication. In fact, no one knows how the plants arrived in the New World. As coffee author Stewart Less Allen says in *The Devil's Cup*, de Clieu gets full marks for having cooked up the best story.

In the French town of Dieppe, it is traditional to toast weddings and baptisms with coffee, not wine. It is believed that this is because French aristocrat Gabriel de Clieu was born here.

Coffee Comes to Brazil

In Brazil, the coffee industry began in 1727 when a Brazilian military man and diplomat, Lt. Col. Francisco de Melo Palheta, brought coffee cherries from French Guyana intent on starting the country's first coffee plantation. Sent under the guise of negotiating a border dispute, Palheta charmed the governor's wife into giving him a farewell bouquet that included the valuable coffee seedlings. It took less than 50 years for coffee to become Brazil's largest cash crop.

Because so much coffee comes from Brazil, you may be surprised to learn that Brazilian coffees are not considered the best in the world. Most Brazilian coffees are somewhat harsh, falling short of greatness.

Almost all the coffee plants grown in the French colonies can be traced back to the tree given to Louis XIV in 1714.

Jamaica Blue Mountain

In 1728, the governor of Jamaica, Sir Nicholas Lawes, received a gift of one coffee plant from the governor of Martinique, none other than Gabriel de Clieu. Some other accounts claim that it was the British who introduced coffee to Jamaica in 1730, where today the most famous and expensive coffee in the world is grown in the Blue Mountains.

Until the late 1800s, most people bought green coffee beans and roasted them at home in a frying pan over an open fire. The United States was the first country to turn to roasted coffee. In many European countries, it was still common to roast at home as late as the 1940s.

COFFEE HISTORY AT A GLANCE (1850–2009)

The Early Days of Coffee in America

- **1850:** James Athearn Folger arrives in San Francisco during the Gold Rush and makes his fortune from coffee; Folgers goes on to become one of the largest companies in North America.
- **1861–65:** During the American Civil War, Union soldiers are given a choice between 8 pounds of ground roasted coffee or 10 pounds of green coffee beans as part of their personal ration of 100 pounds of food.
- **1862:** An American coffee company, Chase & Sanborn, is formed. It is the first coffee company to pack and ship roasted coffee in sealed tins. In a brilliant advertising move, Chase & Sanborn put out a flyer on how to read the coffee grounds at the bottom of the cup like a fortune teller.
- **1864:** American Jabez Burns invents and patents the prototype of a modern coffee roaster. The Burns Company is still manufacturing quality coffee roasting equipment today.
- **1869:** Coffee rust fungus, *Hemileia vastatrix*, appears in Ceylon (present-day Sri Lanka) and, within five years, wipes out the entire East Indies coffee industry—no plantation is left free of the disease.

Arbuckle Bros. Coffee
By 1871, John Arbuckle was considered one of the greatest coffee roasters of his generation. He opened a coffee factory in New York and made millions from his product Ariosa, the first national brand of pre-roasted, packaged coffee.

Arbuckle's coffee was distributed in the age before lined paper bags, and coffee quickly went stale and rancid. It was common and necessary, therefore, to coat coffee beans in a gelatinous matter. "Glazing," as it came to be known, was a way to lengthen coffee's shelf life by keeping air away from the beans.

Sugar-Glazed Beans

Many different compounds were used in the coffee trade. Arbuckle Bros. settled on a sugar-based glaze. They ended up using so much sugar that, rather than giving large profits to other sugar-selling companies, they decided to enter the sugar business for themselves. The Sugar Trust, feeling encroached upon, quid pro quo decided to enter the coffee business to spite Arbuckle.

Lion's Share

For the better part of the early 1880s and 1890s, the Sugar Trust's Lion Coffee brand battled it out with Arbuckle's brands in the courts and the grocery stores of the nation, staging the first great advertising campaign in history.

Eventually, Arbuckle Bros. won the coffee war, and the sugar boys quit the coffee business. Arbuckle remained America's number one brand until John Arbuckle's death in 1912.

"Post"-War Coffee

Arbuckle's heirs sold the business to Mr. Charles William Post, who was putting together a little company by the name of General Foods. Mr. Post joined the Arbuckle brands with the other little roaster, called Maxwell House, that he had just acquired from the Cheek-Neal Coffee Company.

With the advent of the Pure Food & Drug Act in 1906 and the development of better packaging that retained freshness longer, glazing fell out of fashion. Sugar-glazed beans, now referred to as "torrefaction coffee," are still sold in Spain and South America.

Into the 20th Century

- **1881:** The New York Coffee Exchange opens.

- **1892:** Former wholesale grocer Joel Cheek names his popular coffee blend Maxwell House after the hotel in Nashville, Tennessee, where it's served. For many years, until the late 1980s, Maxwell House is the largest-selling coffee in the U.S. It is currently second only to Folgers.

- **1900:** Hills Brothers introduces vacuum-packed, canned coffee, marking the beginning of the end of local roasting shops and coffee mills.

- **1901:** Japanese-American chemist Satori Kato of Chicago develops the first soluble "instant" coffee, which is sold at the Pan American Exposition. Also, Italian Luigi Bezzera invents the first commercial espresso machine to reduce the time his employees take on their coffee breaks.

- **1903:** In Bremen, Germany, coffee importer Ludwig Roselius turns a batch of ruined coffee beans over to researchers, who perfect the process of removing caffeine from the beans without destroying the flavor. He patents Kaffee Hag, the first decaffeinated coffee. In France, it is marketed under the brand name Sanka, short for *sans caféine*—or decaffeinated—in French. Sanka is introduced to the United States in 1923.

- **1906:** An English chemist living in Guatemala notices a powdery condensation forming on the spout of his silver coffee carafe. After some experimentation, he invents the first instant coffee. He goes on to mass-produce his brand Red E Coffee and later immigrates to the United States. His name was George Constant Washington, of no relation to the first president of America.

- **1908:** German housewife Melitta Bentz makes a coffee filter using her son's blotting paper.

1918: The U.S. Army requisitions all of George C. Washington's instant coffee for troops in World War I.

1920: Prohibition goes into effect in United States, and coffee sales boom.

1938: Nestlé introduces Nescafé, an improved instant coffee, in Switzerland just before World War II; Maxwell House follows with its own instant brand. After being asked by Brazil to help find a solution to their coffee surpluses, Nestlé then develops freeze-dried coffee.

1940: The U.S. imports 70 percent of the world's coffee crop.

1942: During World War II, American soldiers are issued instant Maxwell House coffee in their ration kits. Back home, widespread hoarding leads to coffee rationing.

1946: In Italy, Achilles Gaggia perfects his espresso machine. In the U.S., coffee consumption reaches 20 pounds per capita.

1960: The world's best-known coffee farmer, Juan Valdez, and his mule Conchita are debuted by the Colombian Coffee Federation. It is considered one of the most successful marketing campaigns of any commodity in history—over 75 brands and 500 major customers carry 100 percent Colombian coffee products, including Maxwell House, Folgers and Sara Lee.

1965: Boyd Coffee introduces the Flav-R-Flo brewing system, pioneering the cone-and-paper-filter home brewer.

1966: Dutch immigrant Alfred Peet opens Peet's Coffee in Berkeley, California, launching what is considered the beginning of the specialty coffee revolution. He later teaches his coffee-roasting style to Jerry Baldwin, Zev Siegl and Gordon Bowker.

The Juiciest Coffee Tidbit
In 1969, coffee heiress Abigail Folger and three others were stabbed to death in Los Angeles while visiting her friend Sharon Tate in the home of filmmaker Roman Polanski. She and many others were killed by cult leader Charles Manson. She was stabbed 28 times and, allegedly, Folger's dying words were, "You can stop now. I'm already dead."

On a Coffee High

1970: Italian Luigi Goglio invents a one-way valve to let coffee de-gas without contact with oxygen. The valve helps preserve the quality of the coffee and prevents it from becoming stale.

1971: Jerry Baldwin, Zev Siegl and Gordon Bowker open Starbucks in Seattle.

1975: The Black Frost in Brazil decimates the coffee harvest, leading to high prices over the next two years.

1987: Howard Schultz buys Starbucks and begins to turn it into a worldwide specialty coffee chain.

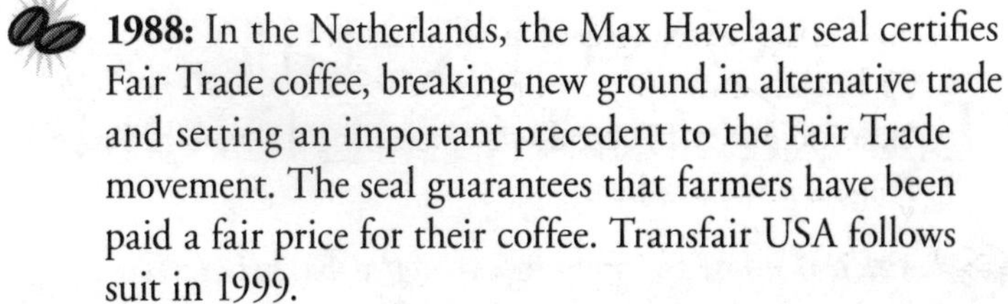

- **1988:** In the Netherlands, the Max Havelaar seal certifies Fair Trade coffee, breaking new ground in alternative trade and setting an important precedent to the Fair Trade movement. The seal guarantees that farmers have been paid a fair price for their coffee. Transfair USA follows suit in 1999.
- **1994:** Rwanda's coffee industry is nearly destroyed during the civil war and genocide.
- **2006:** Specialty coffee accounts for 40 percent of the U.S. retail coffee market.
- **2009:** Starbucks introduces instant coffee in single-serving packets.

DID YOU KNOW?

Today, cigarette giant Philip Morris owns Maxwell House.

Café
in French

SO WHERE DID ESPRESSO COME FROM?

Until 1946, just plain old regular coffee was being served. And then along came espresso. Beautiful, bittersweet espresso. Though it may be made in a hurry, espresso is meant to be savored—and no one knows how to slow down and smell the coffee like Italians. Although it was actually the French who first developed a crude espresso machine, it was the Italians who perfected the coffee craft and became the first to commercially manufacture espresso machines.

The World's First Espresso Machine

In 1946, Achille Gaggia invented the spring piston espresso machine, which was far easier to use and safer than earlier

steam-driven models. It was also the first espresso machine to work without steam.

The Gaggia coffee bar in Italy was also the first location to use these machines and to offer espresso along with their regular coffee. The attractive machines soon spread throughout the cafés in Europe, eventually coining the term "pulling a shot," which referred to the machine's long handle used to push the hot water through the espresso grounds.

Improving Coffee Quality in England

In the 1950s, Italian Pino Riservato, appalled at the quality of the coffee being served in English cafés, brought the first espresso machine from Milan to London. As luck and circumstance would have it, he was related by marriage to a director of Gaggia back in Italy and soon formed Riservato and Partners Ltd. to import Gaggia machines into London. The horse muck they were passing off as coffee could not go on! British coffee standards absolutely had to be improved.

Post-War Coffee Bars

From the beginning, coffee bars represented a new phenomenon in England. Consciously aimed at attracting a young, modern clientele, they were places with interesting and unusual interiors where everyone was welcome.

However, the first five Gaggia machines ordered from Italy arrived without an import license and were refused entry. Understandably, the established catering trade was less than interested in offering better coffee, and the venture seemed doomed from the outset. But in fact, it was this initial disinterest that made coffee bars so unique and eventually helped them thrive. As Edward Bramah points out in his 1972 book *Tea and Coffee*, after the catering trade rejected the Gaggia machine, those who opened coffee bars included "a wine merchant, an interior decorator, an antique dealer, a milliner, not to mention furriers, tailors, dentists, sculptors, psychiatrists and film stars." Bramah's conclusion is that "Perhaps it was a good thing that caterers had refused to use this machine, for had they done so, it might well have been lost amid the conventional and uninteresting decor of an English café."

Moka Bar

It was a Scotsman, Maurice Ross, who established London's first coffee bar, named the Moka Bar, with an architect named Geoffrey Crockett. The bar's design was clean and modern, and the grandiose Italian coffee machine was the dominant visual element of the establishment.

Moka Bar only served black espresso, cappuccino, cakes and sandwiches. The milk for the cappuccino was warmed and frothed separately by steam injection—another novel feature, which prevented a skin from forming—and poured onto the black coffee. Then the foamy, white top was lightly dusted with cocoa powder or cinnamon or a wafer of plain chocolate was added to the drink. In post-war Britain, after wartime severity and rationing, the new coffee bar was a momentous success.

Although traditional machines made equally good coffee, it was Riservato who convinced coffee bar proprietors that the Gaggia was a superior-quality product—a must-have if they were ever going to be taken seriously as coffee aficionados.

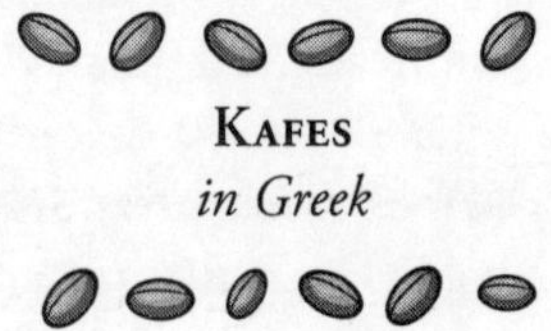

THE SECOND COFFEE HOUSE BOOM

Moka Leads the Way

During its first three years of operation, 300,000 cups of coffee a year were sold in the Moka Bar. By 1960, there were over 2000 coffee bars throughout England, 50 of which were in London.

Corrupting the Youth of England

It became chic to be a server in a coffee bar—they were popular meeting places, especially in the evenings, as they stayed open late. No alcoholic drinks were served and, unlike pubs, women could safely go in alone. Not only that, but the sophisticated coffee bars had jukeboxes loaded up with all the rebellious music of the time, like Elvis!

Adults, naturally, were concerned that the habit of going to coffee bars instead of doing homework was corrupting the youth of England. These "havens" allowed the youths to sit all evening and converse with other teenagers for the low price of a cup of coffee. Inevitably, the coffee bars were suddenly brandished as "houses of ill-repute, where boys smoked and girls were deflowered." Though the complaints may have been justified in certain cases where neighboring gardens were receptacles for cigarette butts and other evidentiary rubber findings, for the most part, the accusations were fear-based and unfounded.

The Coffee Bar Goes Stale

The biggest downfall—and ultimately what led to the ruin of the coffee bar—was their high cost of operation. Not only were the Gaggia machines expensive, but once the novelty had worn off, coffee bars quickly became less profitable. Eventually, cheaper blends of coffee were substituted to bolster profits, and often the machines were not properly maintained. Unless they were regularly cleaned, the coffee took on a stale flavor. The gradual decline brought an end to the second coffee house boom when some coffee bar owners opted for new enterprises such as pizza parlors, which offered quicker cash flow.

The German Coffee Crisis

Although the Germans did not start out as strong coffee drinkers—what with the men making fun of the women and their *Kaffeeklatsch*—Germany did eventually turn into a coffee-drinking nation. In fact, by the 1970s, coffee was one of East Germany's main imports. A massive rise in coffee prices in 1975–77, caused by the Black Frost in Brazil, led to a quadrupling of the annual cost of importing coffee. As a result, in the summer of 1977, the Politburo—the highest decision-making body of the Socialist Unity Party, the ruling communist party in East Germany at the time—pulled most of the cheaper brands of coffee off the shelves, limited its use in restaurants and stopped offering coffee in public offices and state enterprises.

Infamously, a new type of coffee was introduced: *Mischkaffee*. This mixed coffee was an interesting combination of 51 percent coffee and 49 percent "filler," including chicory, rye and sugar beets. Not surprisingly, the new coffee was universally detested for its awful taste. Luckily, the crisis was short-lived and, once coffee prices began to fall in 1978, regular coffee was once again available for public consumption, much to the relief of East Germany's under-caffeinated citizens. Increased supply was also created through an agreement with Vietnam.

Good Morning, Vietnam

In an effort to respond to the coffee crisis, the governments of East Germany and France provided initial funding to Vietnam to help bolster the country's coffee production, which had been steadily growing since the fall of Saigon to the communists in 1975.

The Vietnamese crop is Robusta coffee, a lower quality, less flavorful coffee that is generally processed to meet lower quality standards than the traditional Arabica coffee produced by Latin American growers. Because other Robusta producers (including Indonesia and Brazil) were forced to follow Vietnam's pricing lead, and because the low Robusta prices prompted coffee roasters to use more Robusta in their retail blends, the price problem spread quickly to Arabica coffees as Arabica producers struggled to maintain their share of the coffee market.

Vietnam has become, in just a few short years, the world's second largest exporter of coffee. Since 1995, the growth in Vietnamese coffee production has been explosive, with extensive government funding, an aggressive export promotion program and the government seizure of the ancestral lands of Vietnam's indigenous Montagnard people.

Moreover, because Vietnam's coffee plantations are not "market oriented"—meaning they will sell their coffee regardless of fluctuations in price—they have put ever-increasing quantities of coffee on the world market without any apparent regard for price.

GROWING PAINS

Arabica or Robusta?

Coffee is grown in over 53 countries worldwide, and Brazil is the largest coffee-producing country, with around 30 percent of the world's total output of coffee; Colombia ranks second. Nearly seven million tons of green coffee beans are produced each year worldwide, and coffee growing remains virtually untouched by mechanization.

Over 90 species of the *Coffea* plant (or genus) exist, but just two account for almost all commercial cultivation: *Coffea arabica,* which gives us Arabica coffee, and *Coffea canephora,* which yields Robusta coffee. The Arabica plant is considered to produce the best quality coffee, but it is more prone to disease and can be grown only above an altitude of 2000 feet. The beans of the hardier Robusta are most commonly used in a blend with Arabica, thereby making both yields go farther.

Arabica coffee accounts for around two-thirds of the world's production, but the percentage of Robusta is increasing because it produces better yields. Arabica coffees can be divided into two main categories: those from Brazil, known as "Brazils," and those that come from elsewhere, marked "Other Milds." The two best-known varieties of Arabica are Typica and Bourbon, but many other strains have been developed, including Mundo Novo from Brazil, Caturra from Columbia and Brazil, Tico from Central America and, perhaps most famously, Jamaica Blue Mountain coffee.

Made in the Shade

It takes three to five years for a coffee tree to reach maturity, and it will produce crops for 20 to 30 years, depending on conditions and care. Both Arabica and Robusta varieties require plenty of sun and rain and will die if the temperature falls below freezing. Coffee can be grown anywhere and everywhere, from the smallest of forest clearings to very large estates and on every size of property in between.

Ideally, coffee plants thrive when shaded by neighboring trees. The shade helps conserve the moisture in the soil and protects the developing fruit from the hottest rays of the sun. More modern techniques employ irrigation and fertilizers, but recently, consumer trends have leaned towards supporting more traditional methods.

Coffee comes from the red, ripe fruit of the plants, known as cherries, which take anywhere between six and eleven months to ripen, producing only one harvest per year in most areas. Beneath the red skin of the cherry, there is a fleshy pulp, then a slimy layer, followed by a parchment-like covering of the bean. Inside these layers, coffee cherries usually contain two seeds ("beans") covered in a thin membrane.

Mutation Can Be Good

Coffee cherries usually contain two seeds, except for the "pea-berry" anomaly, when only a single seed is present in the coffee cherry. Approximately five percent of all coffee crops contain peaberries, which are small and round with a tiny crevice that splits them halfway down the middle. Known as *caracol* in Spanish, these little genetic anomalies are prized for their rarity and sweetness and are considered in some circles to be the "caviar of coffees." According to coffee folklore, their superiority is based on the notion that all the good stuff that ordinarily goes into a double bean is squeezed into a single bean.

Some feel that the peaberry tastes no better than other beans in the same crop, though most agree that it does taste a little different. One aficionado described the peaberry as "more buoyant and more brightly acidy, more complex but somewhat lighter in body."

Coffee cherries with three beans are deemed to be a sign of good luck.

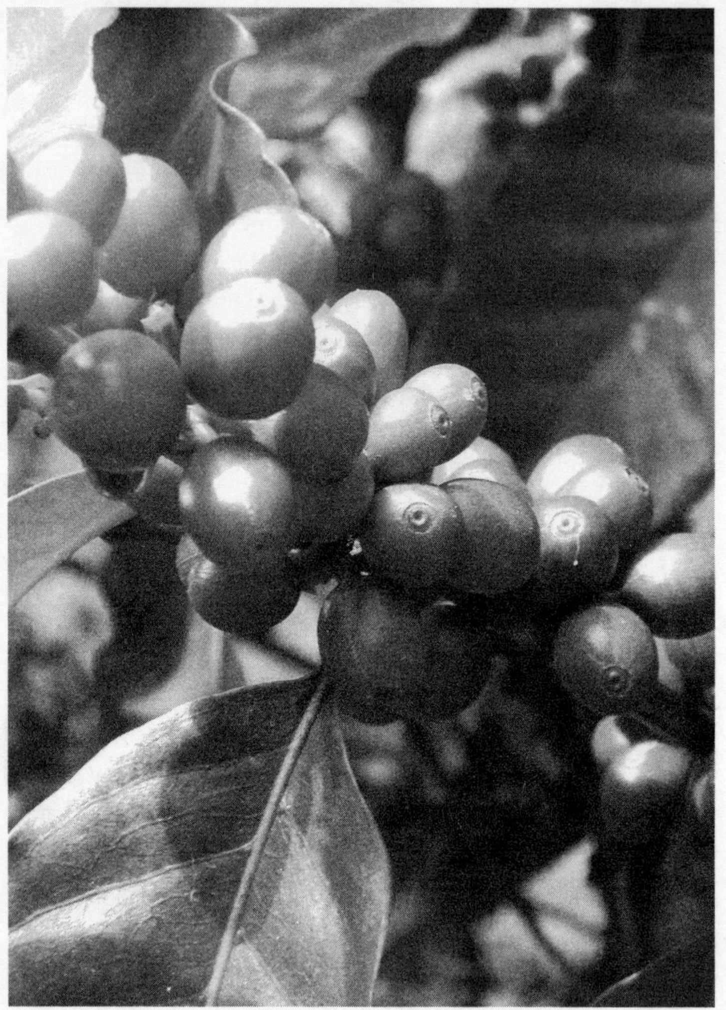

COFFEE BEAN

It's no accident that the highest levels of caffeine in the coffee plant are found in the seeds. They are the most important part of the plant and the high caffeine levels protect the seeds from insects and other predators. So basically, caffeine is nothing more than a natural insecticide.

NOT A BOWL OF CHERRIES

The Rule of Five

According to the Rule of Five, an Arabica coffee plant takes about five years to mature and produce its first crop. A healthy coffee tree will produce only about five pounds of green beans per year, but only about one-fifth of a pound meets the rigid sorting standards to be sold as "specialty coffee."

Most people don't realize what a painstaking method harvesting and processing coffee is. The vast majority of coffee is harvested by hand, and high-quality coffee is even more labor intensive. Beans have four outer layers that must be removed individually, which takes a great deal of time and manpower.

A 100-pound bag of cherries will actually yield only about 20 to 30 pounds of beans—once it is refined, there is close to a 70 percent loss. Roasting reduces the yield still more, to only 11.5 pounds. That, combined with a very unstable coffee market that fluctuates considerably, makes it a wonder that coffee producers make any money at all. It is estimated that the costs of harvesting represent close to half the total annual costs of operating a coffee plantation or a farm. Unfortunately—as is often the case—economics have no effect on the fixed costs involved in producing a quality product or bringing coffee to world markets.

Harvesting

Coffee berries start as green berries in their early stage of growth, and then turn yellow, red and eventually dark crimson at their ripest and finest. Trees blossom over a six- to eight-week period in countries such as Brazil and Mexico, but in countries located along the equator, such as Kenya and Colombia, a coffee tree can have blossoms, ripening fruit and mature cherries all on the branch at the same time.

Coffee is grown on steep terrain and cherries must be carefully picked so that only the ripest are chosen in order to ensure the best quality coffee. Unripe cherries downgrade the overall quality of the coffee. Using ripe cherries also makes pulping and grading easier, since using a mixture of red over- or under-ripe cherries could potentially damage the pulping machine, which is specifically adjusted for the ripe type of red cherry. Because harvesting is so labor intensive, it's also one of the most expensive steps in coffee processing.

The time span between blossoming and harvest generally covers eight to nine months, depending on the altitude and prevailing weather conditions. Arabica, being the oldest species of bean and the most widely cultivated, accounts for 74 percent of the beans grown in the world. Depending on elevation and latitude, the harvesting season for Arabica coffee lasts approximately four months, anytime between September and March.

Stinker Beans

Cherries are generally processed the same day as they are harvested and are never mixed with the previous day's harvest. All equipment and sorting areas need to be thoroughly washed on a daily basis, since any fermented part of cherry from the previous day can contaminate newly harvested cherries and result in the deterioration of the entire batch. Even one rotting bean—known as a stinker—can ruin an entire batch.

Cherries need to be washed and sorted before processing to remove twigs, leaves or other foreign matter. This is an important step that, if skipped, could also jeopardize the market value of the crops.

PROCESSING THE BEANS

A Long Process

This complicated step involves pulping, fermenting, washing, drying, hulling, cleaning, grading, sorting, storing and transporting green beans, and transforms the cherries into lean, green caffeinated machines, ready for roasting or export.

Tired yet? You should be! Processing involves a long chain of activities aimed at achieving a coffee of the highest quality. If any link in the chain is broken (such as over-fermentation, mold-contamination, taints, odors or physical damage to the bean), then that loss in quality can never be regained.

There are two ways to prepare coffee beans for roasting and the method used has a significant effect on the price and the quality of the final beans.

The Dry Method, or Natural Process

This one-step operation is the simplest, cheapest and most traditional method of preparing coffee beans for roasting. It produces unwashed coffee and is normally used for lower-grade beans. The harvested cherries are spread over a flat, sunny surface, where they can be raked regularly to prevent fermentation. The coffee beans are dried inside the unbroken cherries to 12 percent moisture.

It takes approximately four weeks for the cherries to dry. Some expertise is required during this stage, since over-drying the beans may lead to damage during the hulling stage and under-drying them may cause mold. Once dry, the cherries are hulled to produce dry, green beans.

The Wet Method

Arabica beans, since they are of higher quality, are mainly processed using the "wet" method. This process is more expensive since it requires large quantities of water, more equipment and meticulous management, but causes less damage and produces higher-quality coffee.

The main difference between the two methods is that, in the wet method, the pulp is removed from the bean almost immediately instead of allowing the cherries to fully dry first.

Pulping

The pulp is removed in the pulping machine, which crushes the cherries. Pulping must be done as soon as possible after harvesting—no later than 24 hours—in order to maximize the quality of the beans. If the beans are left too long before processing, the pulpy flesh softens, which makes bean separation difficult and increases the likelihood of damaging the beans.

The beans, now in only their husks, or parchment—a thin, crumbly skin that remains on the beans after they have been de-pulped and dried—are separated from the cherry skin and pulp, which are washed away with water. The washing channels are designed to separate the lighter, immature beans from the heavier, mature ones.

Special machines, such as the Aagaard pre-grader, have been invented to simplify the pulping process. The what? The who? Aagaard was a Norwegian coffee grower who designed the system while working in Kenya. It involves shaking the beans through a sieve into a tank of water. The larger, heavier and riper beans sink through the water first; the lighter ones are carried farther along the tank. This system is well liked since the water in this process can be recycled and the parchment produced is well pulped and of a uniform size.

Fermentation

At this stage, the beans still have a sugary coating of pulp—unfortunately known as mucilage—which is then left to ferment in tanks over the next several days. The parchment, which acts as a protective coating, is dried for anywhere between 12 and 36 hours, depending on conditions such as temperature, thickness of the mucilage and the rate of fermentation. When the process is complete, the parchment is dry and rough and then is washed thoroughly to remove all traces of fermented mucilage. (Thank goodness!)

Semi-Wash Alternative

There is a third processing method known as the "semi-wash," which is a combination of the wet and dry methods.

Demucilager—Ew!

The skin of the fresh cherry is removed by a pulping machine and water (as in the wet method) but then the remaining fruit is left to dry on the beans rather then being washed off (as in the dry method). This process does not ferment the mucilage since it is mechanically removed immediately after pulping using a machine called a demucilager. The clean parchment is ready for drying as soon as the demucilager has done its dirty work.

The Happy Medium

Originally used in Brazil in the 1990s, the semi-wash method has been considered a great success in countries like India, where it has helped to upgrade the quality of the bean in a cost-effective manner without the need for fermentation and washing.

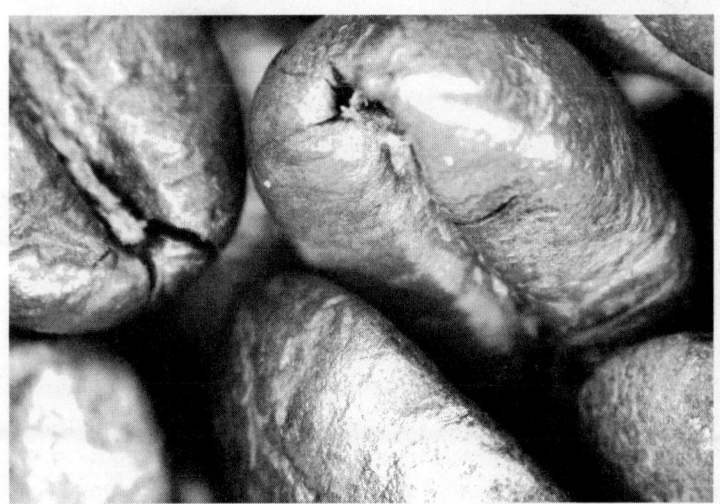

The pulper and demucilager units are cheaper, use less water, reduce the risk of over-fermentation and therefore deliver a higher-quality product than simply using the dry method.

The resulting coffee has increased body and sweetness, while smoothing out any earthy notes left by the traditional drying method. In other words, your coffee won't taste like dirt.

Drying the Beans

Did you have any idea that Arabica beans were so finicky? They could give a diva a run for her money. The parchment has to be dried to around 11 percent moisture so the beans can be stored in a stable condition. If Arabica beans are over-dried to 10 percent, they lose their blue-green color and some of their quality, whereas too much moisture causes mold.

Mechanical dryers are used on some of the larger plantations or where rain could spoil the drying. In most cases, however, the beans are better left in the sun for 12 to 15 days, where they are turned regularly to ensure even drying. It's important that the parchment doesn't crack, so if the sun is too strong, the beans need to be covered.

Storing the Beans

Because beans are exported year round and not just during the harvesting period, the protective parchment on the coffee helps keep the beans stable and of the freshest quality.

A green bean that is stored for a long period of time in hot and humid conditions will absorb moisture from the atmosphere. Humidity of over 70 percent will damage the beans, so they aren't often stored on the farms that produce them. To ensure minimum spoilage, beans in jute sacks or woven poly bags should be evenly stacked in a well-ventilated area. Arabica beans should not be stored for more than 12 months, but Robusta beans can be stored a little longer, though eventually both varieties will begin to fade and mottle.

Hulling: The End of a Long Haul

Just before it is exported, the coffee beans are hulled, which means that the parchment—which has until now shielded the delicate bean—will finally be removed.

Different hullers are used depending on the processing method, since the parchment on wet-processed coffee beans is harder to remove than that of dry-processed beans. There are a range of machines that are able to clean and sort hulled coffee by color, size, density and—believe it or not—aerodynamic shape. Are we making coffee here, or spaceships?

And, of course, hulling—like the rest of coffee production—is a tedious and precise process. If the huller is set incorrectly or the coffee is over-dry and brittle, coffee beans can be damaged; alternatively, if the coffee is too wet, the beans can easily be crushed.

In the end (and yes, we're almost there) no machine is as effective as the human eye, which is used in the final process to hand sort the coffee that is otherwise ready for export.

Polishing

Polishing removes any of the remaining silver skin from the green beans after the hulling process. In the past, polished beans were considered superior to unpolished ones. Today, some connoisseurs believe that polishing actually detracts from the cup by over-refining the beans. The truth is that there is hardly any discernable difference in taste between the two.

Grading and Sorting

Coffee beans are graded in various ways. Before any coffee is sold or roasted, it is classified by the number of defects, size and

shape, color, region or cultivar and cup quality. Grading experts are trained to know their beans—they can tell a good bean from a bad one and know exactly how good your coffee will be before it ever reaches your cup.

Size Matters!

Beans are graded first by size and then by density. Generally, larger beans produce better coffee. Size is rated on a scale of 10 to 20, though some are given letter grades according to size. For example, Kenyan coffees are graded as A, B and C, with AA being the best coffee.

The Maragogype is a specialty hybrid Arabica bean that is naturally larger and therefore commands a premium price.

Getting Sized Up

Beans are sized by being filtered through a sieve, but even beans of the same size can have different weights, and all damaged or shriveled beans need to be removed. Of course, there are some high-tech sorting machines, but the simplest way to separate them is by weight, using gravity as it was intended.

Stinkers Be Gone!

After sorting heavy beans from light beans, the next stage is to get rid of all the defects—any bean with a generally poor appearance is considered a defect. Flaky, poorly roasted, foul-tasting, smelly beans, as well as ones that have been ruined by bad preparation, get the dubious "defective" moniker.

Beans that fail to roast are known as "quakers." Lighter than other roasted beans, quakers are a big reason why bad coffee tastes *bad*. Stinkers (beans that get stuck in the pulper or fermentation tank for too long), blacks (immature or dead cherries that are mistakenly harvested), foxes (improperly washed, over-dried or over-ripe coffee cherries) and sours are just a few of the other names for imperfect beans that are rejected. The defects are tossed, along with any over-fermented or un-hulled beans.

Country by Country

Different countries grade their beans according to different systems. In Costa Rica and Brazil, coffees are graded as Strictly Hard Bean—the highest quality—followed by Good Hard Bean, Hard Bean, Medium Hard Bean, High Grown Atlantic, Medium Grown Atlantic and Low Grown Atlantic.

Coffee beans from Colombia are labeled as Supremo, Excelso, Extra and, the lowest grade, Pasilla.

AT MARKET

Coffee buyers look for beans that are clean and dry. If the beans don't meet their rigorous standards and are wet or have sticks and other debris mixed in, farmers risk losing the whole sale. In this case, the farmers have done all the work, but because they didn't incorporate this one extra nitpicky step, it will end up costing them money, which could have devastating consequences for the next growing season.

Coyote Ugly

Farmers bring their beans to local markets to sell. If their beans are "ugly"—if the cherries are under- or over-ripe, poorly washed, improperly sorted or dried, fermented, misshapen—they end up in the hands of a "coyote." Coyotes are coffee buyers looking to purchase coffee at very low prices, often paying the farmer less than a living wage. This can be devastating, especially after the farmer has gone through all the time and effort to process the coffee beans.

Since most farmers have neither the time nor the resources to take their coffee to markets in bigger centers to try and get a fair price, it is the coyotes who profit from selling the cheaply bought coffee beans in those centers. Farmers can't truck the coffee out and make the deal, so they have to sell to the coyotes. These substandard beans are sold to local and multinational coffee companies that have lower standards for the beans they buy.

So, the next time you raise a cup, take a sip in reverence for all the hard work that went into that finicky little diva bean that provides your daily caffeine fix.

DID YOU KNOW?

There are two major coffee markets in the world. The one in London deals with the buying of Robusta coffee, while the other—known as the Coffee, Sugar and Cocoa Exchange—is in New York. The "C" contract market, as it is known, is a futures market that handles the trade of Arabica coffee.

Cafea
in Rumanian

ROASTING AND CUPPING

Roasting and cupping are considered to be a fine art, and it is said that great coffee depends on these two very important steps in the coffee bean's journey to your lips.

Roasting Coffee

Roasting is the art of coaxing oils that are locked inside the bean to come out and play. The more oil, the stronger the flavor.

Green coffee beans must be exposed to heat before being ground and brewed. During roasting, the bean's sugars are caramelized, which contributes color, body, sweetness, complexity and flavor to the cup. The level—that is, the length of time the beans are heated—is categorized as the roast. Listed in order from lightest to darkest, the following are the roast levels most commonly encountered in retail coffee:

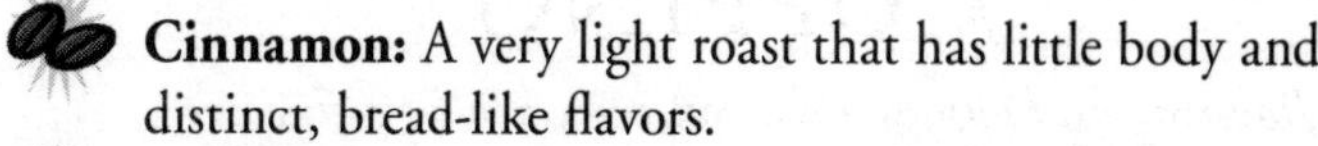

- **Cinnamon:** A very light roast that has little body and distinct, bread-like flavors.
- **City:** A light roast, distinguished by its milk-chocolate color, which reflects coffee's natural flavor characteristics.
- **Full City:** A medium roast in which the coffee's oils, which form naturally as a result of chemical reactions that take place during the roasting process, begin to show on the surface of the brewed cup.
- **Vienna:** The lightest of the dark roasts, but the first in which the roast becomes noticeable in the taste. When brewed, the coffee has a rich brown color and reveals more oil on the surface.
- **French:** The roast, not the coffee bean, is the dominant element in French-roast coffee, which has a deep flavor that is both acidic and smoky.
- **Italian:** One of the darkest grades available, this coffee tastes almost exclusively of the roast.

DID YOU KNOW?

A lot of moisture is lost during roasting, which means that beans weigh less after roasting than before. The bean also loses some of its protein and about 10 to 15 percent of its caffeine.

Simple...In Theory

Proper roasting is about keeping the beans moving to make sure they do not burn. It sounds simple, but the most important stage of the process comes in the phase known as cooling, or quenching.

A good roaster needs to know the exact right moment to stop roasting the beans.

Coffee that is not roasted long enough or at a hot enough temperature to bring out the oil has a pasty, nutty or bread-like flavor. Alternatively, coffee roasted too long or at too high a temperature will taste burned and takes on an industrial flavor. We've all no doubt had the misfortune at one point or another of having a cup of very badly burnt coffee—it tastes like old sneakers left on a radiator. Over-roasting has the same effect. On the other hand, coffee roasted too long at too low a temperature has a baked flavor.

How It's Done

During the early stage of roasting, the color of the bean will not change too much and will generally remain light brown in color since the oil has not been volatilized.

Cracking Beans

When the inside of the bean reaches a temperature of about 400°F, the oil suddenly appears. The beans begin to "crack" and develop oils in a process called "pyrolysis," which is just geek-speak for saying that the beans start to turn brown.

The Moment of Truth

This is where the expertise of a roastmaster is most needed. When the beans "crack" a second time, they are dumped from the roaster and cooled immediately. The coffee essence must be stopped at exactly the right moment to allow for pyrolysis but to prevent burning. This is where the flavor is truly captured, the combination of aroma, acidity and body. Allowing the beans to cool at room temperature will mean that they may still over-roast.

Air or Water Quenching

With smaller-scale equipment, the cooling can be done by fans that pull room-temperature air through the hot beans while they are stirred, a procedure called air quenching. Larger roasting machines allow the roastmaster to water-quench the beans, kicking off the cooling process with a brief spray of water. If the water quenching is done properly, the water evaporates immediately from the surface of the hot beans and does not negatively affect the flavor of the coffee. In fact, coffee that has been properly water-quenched often tastes better than air-quenched coffee because the cooling is more immediate.

The chemistry of coffee roasting is complex and still not completely understood. This is owing to the variety of beans, as well as to the complexity of the coffee essence, which still defies chemists' best efforts to duplicate it in the laboratory.

Cupping Coffee

Cupping coffees is one of the most unique aspects of the coffee world. Cupping is simply coffee talk for tasting coffee—the act of assessing the qualities of a particular batch of beans by freshly roasting, brewing and tasting it. It is work for serious and talented professionals and involves intense focus punctuated by noisy, explosive slurps. As one cupper explains, it might look and sound silly, but it's a very effective way to taste!

When coffee is "cupped," its quality and flavor profile is evaluated using very precise sensory criteria. For cupping, coffees are roasted only very lightly so that the nuances of the coffee's own flavors and aromas aren't obscured by the roasting process. According to the folks at Green Mountain Coffee, cuppers then grind and brew these coffees in open bowls and judge their merits on the following qualities:

Fragrance: This is the smell of the newly ground coffee before it's brewed. The coffee's fragrance can speak volumes about the its origin and the care of its processing.

Aroma: The smell of the brewed coffee is evaluated. Coffee's aromas vary dramatically from origin to origin. Some have floral qualities, others offer the smell of citrus and fruit, even wood and earth.

Acidity: This is the bright and dry taste that adds life to a coffee. Kenyan and any wet-processed coffees are known for being very acidic. Acidic coffee won't upset your stomach; instead, it will make your taste buds tingle. Bright coffees offer a pleasing tang on the tongue. Acidity, though, is not the same as bitterness. Bitterness in coffee usually comes from skimping on grounds when you brew, brewing for too long, or—perish the thought—brewing in a pot or machine with coffee that was ground hours, days or weeks ago.

Flavor: The diversity in coffee's flavor from origin to origin is astounding—even coffees from the same origin can sometimes taste different based on their growing conditions and processing method.

Body: This is the measure of the richness of the coffee taste. Longer roasting yields more body, but it also decreases acidity, which is the tingly taste on your tongue. Full-bodied coffees may be buttery or even syrupy, and there is a definite tradeoff between body and acidity.

Finish: The sensations that remain in the mouth after the coffee is swallowed—its aftertaste—is called the finish. Some coffees impart a sweet, lingering finish; others are more direct, even abrupt.

Balance: This is how all the coffee's individual flavors and taste sensations come together. Balance tends to separate good coffees from great coffees, in which the overall composition is somehow greater than the sum of its parts.

Throughout the evaluation process, cuppers also need to take into account *where* a particular coffee is from. As one expert states,

"Qualities that are highly desirable in an American coffee—bright, citrus aromas and clean, polished flavors—are not the same qualities that are desired in coffees from Indonesia, where a more muted acidity and a lush, lyrical body is the norm."

Having the palate and the knowledge to differentiate between all these different nuances culminates in one great cupper.

How Bad Is It?

Defective or undesirable coffee flavors include earthiness and wildness, which is described using many different terms: gamey, musty, earthy, groundy, harsh, sour, grassy, hidey, barnyard, fermented, skunked or "Rioy," which is a term given to the cheaper, harsher sour-tasting coffees reminiscent of the coffee that used to come out of Rio de Janeiro.

In general, if the coffee tastes like dirt or is "gamey" (meaning the coffee has a bad taste that can't necessarily be identified), cuppers will want to avoid it at all costs. "Musty" means the coffee tastes like mildew, "fermented" means the coffee tastes like alcohol, and "hidey" means it tastes like it was kept in leather or a tanned hide.

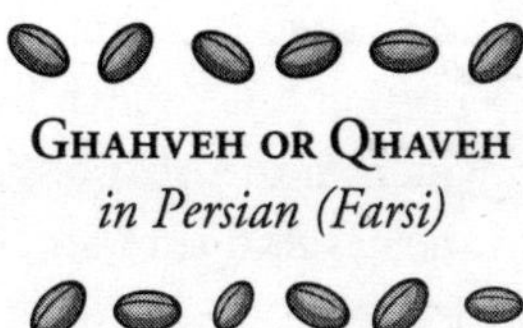

STORING AND MAKING COFFEE

The powers of a man's mind are directly proportioned to the quantity of coffee he drinks.
–Sir James Mackintosh, Scottish historian and statesman

Storing Beans

If you have to store coffee for longer than a week, keep it in the freezer in an airtight container. The beans can go straight from the freezer into a grinder. It is always best to have whole beans and grind them at home just before brewing your coffee.

Coffee's Enemies

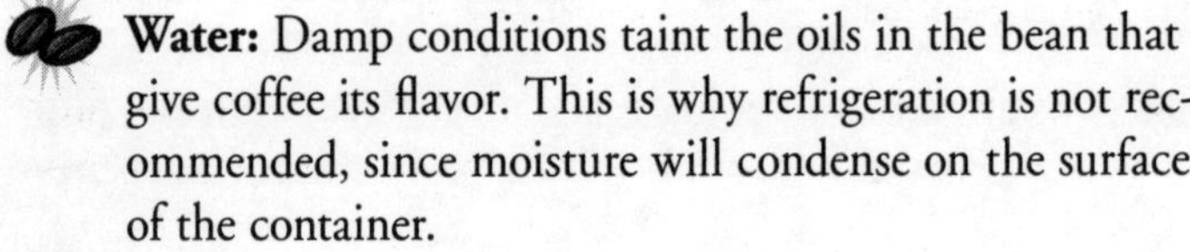

- **Water:** Damp conditions taint the oils in the bean that give coffee its flavor. This is why refrigeration is not recommended, since moisture will condense on the surface of the container.
- **Oxygen:** It is important to grind the beans just before you brew because oxygen oxidizes the volatile flavors. Once coffee has been ground, much more of its surface is exposed to air, which means that oils begin to evaporate and the flavor vanishes into thin air.
- **Air, Heat and Light:** Each of these factors impairs the flavor of coffee, so the fresher the beans, the richer and more flavorful the cup. Store beans in an airtight container in a cool, dry place.

Coffee quickly picks up other scents and flavors, so do not store it near any strong-smelling or strong-flavored product unless you feel like an onion- or salami-flavored cup of joe.

Making a Perfect Cup of Coffee

There is no single "best" method of making coffee. The best method is whichever suits the drinker. According to Jon Thorn, author of *The Coffee Companion*, there are six simple rules to observe if you want to make a good cup of coffee every time, no matter the method:

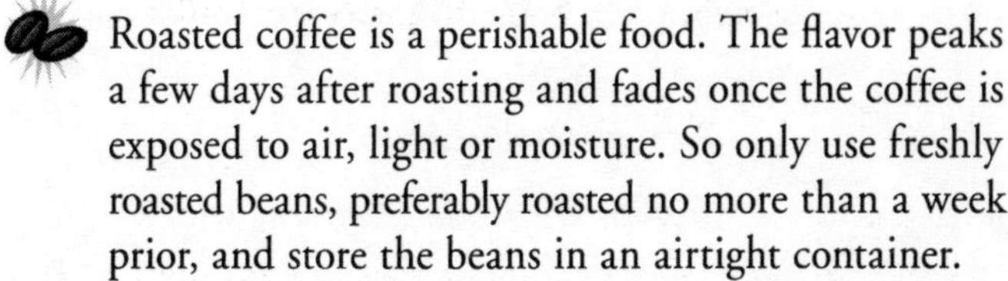

- Roasted coffee is a perishable food. The flavor peaks a few days after roasting and fades once the coffee is exposed to air, light or moisture. So only use freshly roasted beans, preferably roasted no more than a week prior, and store the beans in an airtight container.

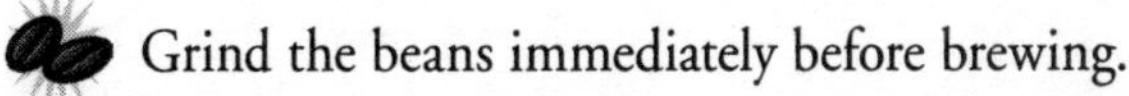

- Grind the beans immediately before brewing.
- Use fresh, cold water drawn from a tap that has been allowed to run for a few seconds. Bring water to the boil but do not over-boil and do not pour boiling water on the coffee.

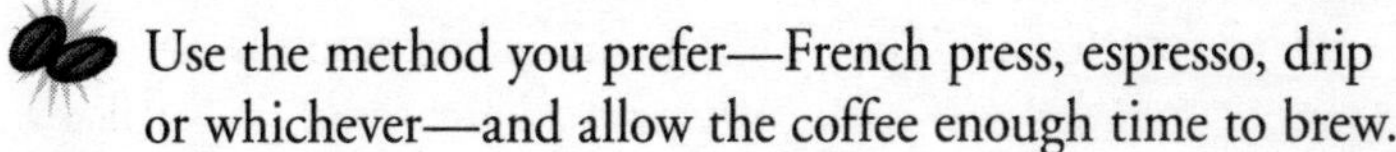

- Use the method you prefer—French press, espresso, drip or whichever—and allow the coffee enough time to brew.
- Drink the freshly brewed coffee as soon as possible (which shouldn't be a problem for most of us.)
- Remember to warm your cup or mug before you pour in the coffee.

Coffee comes in five descending stages: Coffee, Java, Jamoke, Joe, and Carbon Remover.
–Robert A. Heinlein, author of *Glory Road*

Bean There, Done That...

Today, there are dozens of ways to prepare coffee, but there is still a fundamental difference between all of these methods and the traditional Arabian way, in which coffee is boiled three times. Boiling coffee is just plain bad, because it burns off the caffeol, affecting flavor and aromas and rendering the brew bitter. To overcome this, the Arabs traditionally added cardamom to their coffee, but no matter—the Arabian way of making coffee never did catch on.

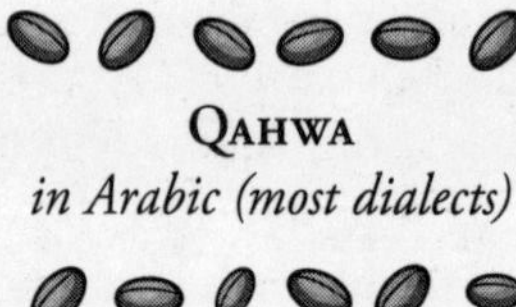

Qahwa
in Arabic (most dialects)

COFFEE TALK

The Art of Espresso

Espresso is a single, one-ounce shot of coffee made with seven grams of finely ground coffee extracted between 18 and 25 seconds. The coffee is denser and more intense because hot water is forced through the grounds at high pressure. Sound simple? The truth is that making quality espresso is an art. In fact, it is possibly the most difficult and potentially the most expensive way to make coffee.

There is some debate about the word's origin. Some say that espresso comes from the French word *exprès*, meaning "especially for" because the drink is made especially for one person. Others believe espresso comes from the Italian verb *expresere*, which means "to press out" or "to put under pressure," which is exactly how the beverage is made.

The Importance of Tamping

Correctly tamped coffee grounds result in more even water distribution, which allows the full espresso flavor to be extracted. Incorrect tamping can cause uneven extraction, leading to bitterness and loss of flavor. Many modern espresso machines are now designed to take E.S.E. (Easy Serving Espresso) pods, which, although more costly and less fresh, take the guesswork out of measuring and tamping and produce a consistent cup of espresso every time.

Under Pressure

The amount of exertion is the key. Once the correct quantity of ground coffee has been dosed into the filter basket and there is an even coffee surface, a hand tamper should be used for the initial tamp, exerting around five pounds of pressure. After tapping the basket gently to knock off any loose grounds, 30 pounds of pressure needs to be applied for the finishing tamp. Before releasing the pressure, the tamper should be rotated a couple of times to smooth the surface.

So how do baristas know the right amount of pressure to apply? Practice! And some even admit to practicing with a hand tamper on a bathroom scale to get a feel for the correct pressure of a finishing tamp.

Crema: The Sign of a Good Cup

Crema is a golden-brownish foam that covers a freshly brewed cup of espresso. It is created by the oils in the coffee mixing with water and air during the extraction process. Experts say that a thick and properly poured layer of crema is a vital indication of the quality of a cup of espresso. This artistic achievement helps keep the heat and aroma in the espresso, and it should be evenly colored. A dark brown crema with a white dot or black hole in the middle is a sign that the espresso has been over-extracted and will taste harsh and bitter. A light-colored crema, on the other hand, means a weak, under-extracted espresso.

The Four Ms

The espresso-brewing method is said to be defined by the four Ms: *miscela* is the mixture of coffee, or blend; *macinazione* is the correct grinding of the coffee blend; *macchina* is the machine that is used; and *mano* is the skilled hand of the barista.

Espresso has one-third the caffeine of a regular cup of coffee. Caffeine content goes up as the water spends more time in contact with the grounds. Brewing espresso takes less than 25 seconds, while other methods take several minutes. Lighter roasts also have a higher caffeine content than darker roasts.

Say It Right, Wouldja

Did you know that many people still ask for a cup of "expresso," instead of espresso. In many places, if you order an expresso, you will be politely ignored.

Espresso Drinks

The espresso shot forms the basic ingredient for many other well-known coffee creations:

- **Americano ("American"):** an espresso shot diluted with hot water to taste
- **Corretto ("correct, proper"):** espresso shot with grappa, an Italian grape brandy
- **Doppio ("double"):** a double shot of espresso
- **Iced espresso:** a double shot of espresso over crushed ice

 **Lungo ("long"):** an espresso made by extracting about 1.5 ounces of water through 7 grams of coffee; the texture is thinner, but it contains a greater amount of caffeine

 **Macchiato ("marked, stained"):** a cup of espresso that is "marked" with a spoonful of the foam from steamed milk, whereas a latte macchiato is a cup of steamed milk "marked" with a small dash of espresso

 **Ristretto ("restricted"):** a more concentrated espresso, normally of only about 0.75 ounces, made by restricting the extraction time, maximizing the flavor of the coffee and minimizing the caffeine

 **Romano ("Roman"):** an espresso shot served with a twist of lemon

Cappuccino: It's All About the Milk

Ideally, a cappuccino is one-third espresso, one-third milk and one-third froth. A really good cappuccino is even more difficult to make than espresso.

If you go to Italy and order a coffee, you will be served a porcelain mug of perfection. You'll drink it, have a mini religious experience and come home raving about the World's Best Coffee. Here's the thing—it's not all about the coffee. It was the milk that made it taste so heavenly.

The main challenge in perfecting the cappuccino lies in preparing the milk, which must not be allowed to boil, or its chemical character will alter and affect the overall flavor. Full fat, slightly caramelized milk that has been steamed to perfection will produce a velvety texture and a natural sweetness that is unparalleled.

Full Steaming Ahead

Steaming milk should happen in two distinct stages: stretching and spinning. Stretching introduces air into the milk via the steam wand to increase its volume, while spinning involves whipping the steamed milk into the desired velvety texture by keeping the liquid in motion, swirling it as it is steamed.

The secret to great steamed milk—start with cold milk. Not only does cold milk foam better, but the foam lasts longer and tastes fresher. Using a cold frothing tin will also will turn the milk into foam more quickly.

DID YOU KNOW?

Chocolate sprinkled on a cappuccino has a purpose. It actually stops a skin from forming on the cappuccino if the milk has been allowed to boil.

The First Cappuccino Machines

The cappuccino is certainly a dramatic and impressive drink, and so is the machine that makes it. The original cappuccino machines were true works of art. These massive, ornate and imposing steam machines were designed to brew coffee and foam milk in a stimulating and entertaining ritual. Much of the enjoyment of this exotic Italian classic was watching the skill and showmanship that went into every cup.

DID YOU KNOW?

Cappuccino is so called because it is the same color as the habit of the Capuchin friars, a religious order founded in the 16th century. The name refers to the long, pointed cowl, or hood, that is worn as part of the order's habit, which is a tasty caramel color.

The Coffee Olympics

Thermometers, steaming pitchers, tampers and knockboxes are some of the essentials needed to make a great cup of espresso.

Professional baristas practice for years to achieve the perfect espresso and cappuccino, perhaps in the hopes of the chance to participate in the World Barista Championship, the so-called "Olympics" of coffee, which take place every year. Just like the real Olympics, the host city changes every year; past cities have included Copenhagen, Denmark; Tokyo, Japan; and Berne, Switzerland.

Strong Competition

At the U.S. Barista Championships, coffee is taken very seriously. Here are a few examples of some of the criteria that baristas are evaluated on:

 The taste of the espresso (harmonious balance of sweet/acidic/bitter)

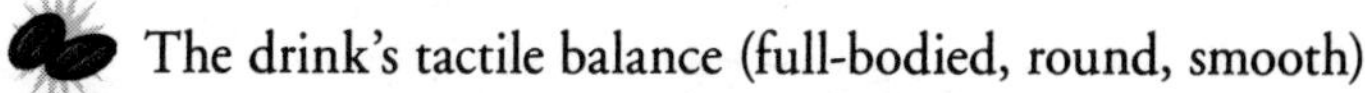

- The drink's tactile balance (full-bodied, round, smooth)
- The taste of the cappuccino
- The taste balance (served at an acceptable temperature, a harmonious balance of rich, sweet milk and espresso)
- The visual correctness of the cappuccino
- An acceptable amount of milk waste at the end of the process
- The color of the crema; the consistency and persistence of the crema

Café Latte

The terms café latte and café au lait both refer to the same drink, though in North America it has become standard to simply say "latte." Much milkier than a cappuccino, it contains one part espresso with at least five parts steamed milk and only a small amount of froth on top.

Variations on the latte theme include the following:

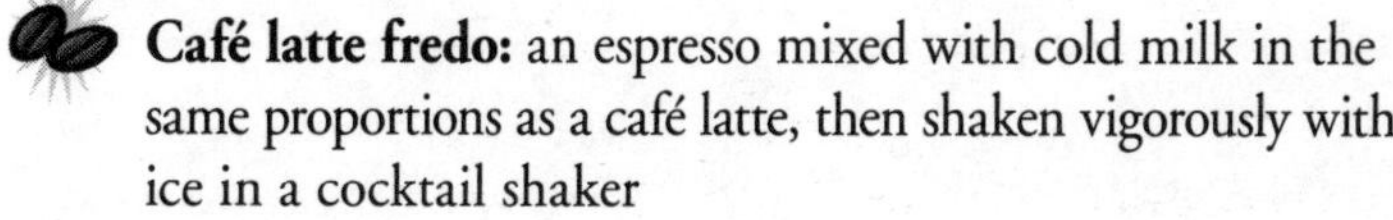

- **Café latte fredo:** an espresso mixed with cold milk in the same proportions as a café latte, then shaken vigorously with ice in a cocktail shaker
- **Café mocha:** one part espresso with one part chocolate syrup and two or three parts frothed milk, optionally topped with whipped cream
- **Espresso con panna:** one shot of espresso topped with a small amount of whipped cream
- **Espresso granita:** one shot of espresso mixed with a teaspoon of soft brown sugar and a splash of brandy, then frozen, crushed and served in a parfait glass with whipped cream

Frappuccino

The frappuccino was invented to rescue declining afternoon coffee sales in California. Since nobody was interested in drinking hot coffee during the hottest part of the day, Starbucks manager Greg Rogers came up with the ice-cold, blended coffee drink in 1994.

Starbucks didn't even create the name. The name frappuccino was trademarked years before by a Boston coffee shop chain called Coffee Connection. Starbucks soon bought out Coffee Connection and started using the name frappuccino.

Starbucks' research and development department tries to anticipate which colors will be hot in the fashion world a year from now, so that future frappuccino flavors will match the outfits of trendy customers.

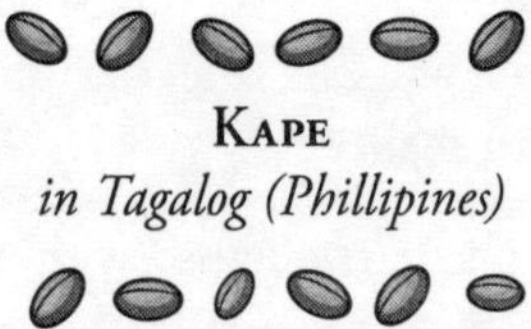

DECAFFEINATION

Decaffeinated coffee is kind of like kissing your sister.
–Bob Irwin

What Have They Done to My Coffee?

To sell a coffee as decaffeinated, it must be at least 97 percent caffeine free. Decaffeination begins with the green bean and is usually done in the same place where the coffee is roasted, prior to roasting. Early processes included steaming the beans to open them, soaking them in a solvent of noxious chemicals such as chloroform or benzene to destroy the caffeine, then steaming them again to eliminate residual traces of the solvent. Who knew decaf could be such a toxic brew?

Later, the coffee industry turned to methylene chloride. Although some of the big U.S. roasters have since abandoned the chemical, the Food and Drug Administration actually still allows its use in the United States as long as residues fall below certain limits. Yikes.

The European Community recently banned the use of methylene chloride for coffee decaffeination. Although measures are taken to ensure that much of the toxic chemical is recycled, some of the evaporated vapors that escape into the atmosphere during processing can be harmful to the ozone layer.

Decaffeination can also be achieved using a carbon dioxide process, a complex water process or by replacing the methylene chloride with ethyl acetate, which is a less harmful chemical.

Water Decaffeination

Have you ever heard of the Swiss Water Process? Well, then you know all about water decaffeination, which is exactly the same thing.

Start by soaking coffee beans in water and letting the liquid drain off. Next, throw the coffee away. What? Although it may seem counter-intuitive, the coffee has now become flavorless. It is the liquid that is now full of both the coffee flavors and the caffeine.

Next, pass the liquid through a carbon filter, which removes the caffeine but keeps the flavor, and pour it into a new batch of coffee. Presto! You have yourself a cup of decaf! Because the liquid is already full of coffee flavors, no more additional flavor is needed from the coffee beans. This cycle of soaking and filtering out the caffeine can be repeated indefinitely.

Since no chemicals are used, no residual chemicals are left in the beans. This is good for the body and better for the environment, and some tasters are convinced that the water process produces a slightly more flavorful cup of coffee.

You Get What You Pay For

Unfortunately, water decaffeinated coffee is much more expensive. In fact, Swiss Water Processed coffee is as much as four times as expensive as other conventionally decaffeinated coffees. For this reason, the only roasters who use it are those whose customers can afford to be sensitive to health and environmental issues.

Carbon Dioxide Decaffeination

In the carbon dioxide (CO_2) decaffeination process, water-soaked coffee beans are placed in a stainless steel container, or extractor, which is then sealed and into which liquid CO_2 is injected. The CO_2 acts as a solvent, dissolving and drawing the caffeine from the coffee beans.

The caffeine-laden CO_2 is then transferred to another container. Here, the pressure is released, and the CO_2 returns to its gaseous state, leaving the caffeine behind. The caffeine-free CO_2 gas is pumped back into a pressurized container for reuse. CO_2 decaffeination produces the most flavorful decaffeinated coffee, and there are no harmful chemicals or by-products left behind by this process.

Unfortunately, the cost of building a CO_2 decaffeination plant is quite high, so this process is primarily used to decaffeinate large volumes of commercial-grade coffee. Because of the growing market for a safe and flavorful decaffeinated product, CO_2 decaffeinated specialty-grade coffees are becoming more readily available. There is at least one CO_2 decaffeination plant in Germany that has been organically certified and can decaffeinate specialty-grade coffees in relatively small quantities.

Growing Decaf

Attempts have been made to grow a naturally uncaffeinated coffee variety, but unfortunately, no caffeine also equals no taste. Scientists have been diligently working on a bio-engineered Arabica strain that will have all the flavor and none of the caffeine, but have made little progress in the past 15 years.

It's not really a big deal, I guess, seeing as less than 15 percent of all the coffee consumed in the United States is decaf.

Sticking It to Coffee

Recently, there has been a new invention that sucks caffeine from already-brewed coffee.

Biochemist Anna Leone was on a transatlantic flight, doing what most of us do in airplanes—homework on molecular polymers—when she was told that she could not get a decaf coffee. She started musing, as so many of us do, about the theory of molecular polymers that can recognize certain molecules, "grab" them and pull them out of a mixed substance.

Well, we'll just have to take her word for it.

By the time she landed, she had the product idea. Now, the DeCaf Company of San Francisco has come up with a wand-like instrument that literally stirs the caffeine from a drink.

Turns out that its not an entirely new idea. Klaus Mosbach, founder of the Centre for Molecular Imprinting in Sweden, did similar research for Unilever some years ago with the intention of finding a powder that would neutralize the caffeine in drinks. It was never marketed because it couldn't remove enough caffeine to make a difference.

The Coffee Research Institute in America has said that the main difference between conventional decaffeination and the new stick is that existing decaffeination methods irrevocably change the flavor of the coffee, whereas the DeCaf stick doesn't affect the flavor in the least.

The DeCaf sticks may soon be appearing in restaurants, right next to the ketchup. Another interesting development is the technology's potential to remove alcohol from a drink, though why would anyone want to do that? Maybe they should invent a stir-stick that can swirl out date-rape drugs.

INSTANT COFFEE

All Dried Up

Compared to the throes of decaffeination, making instant coffee is a relatively simple process. No strange chemicals or noxious gases need to be used—essentially, instant coffee is just regularly brewed coffee with nearly all the water removed.

There are two methods for producing instant coffee: freeze-drying and spray-drying.

Freeze-Drying

The freeze-drying method preserves the most coffee flavor, but it's a more involved process. First, the brewed coffee is allowed to sit until the water evaporates naturally, leaving behind a concentrated coffee solution. This concentrate is then frozen to around –40°F (–40°C) so that any remaining water freezes into ice crystals. Sublimation (a natural process similar to evaporation that transforms a solid into a gas without an intervening liquid stage) is used to remove the ice, resulting in dry grains of brewed coffee. Just add hot water and *voila!*—coffee in your cup!

Spray-Drying

The second method is spray-drying. The water is again allowed to evaporate from the brewed coffee first, forming a concentrate. The concentrated coffee is then sprayed from a high tower into a large hot-air chamber—as the droplets fall, the remaining water evaporates, letting the dry coffee crystals fall to the bottom of the chamber where they can be collected. The high temperatures involved in this method, though, do tend to affect the oils in the coffee and more of the flavor is lost.

Although some people may consider dehydrating coffee to be the "death of the bean," instant coffee can be skillfully used for cooking, baking or cocktailing.

Where Did Instant Coffee Come From?

It all began with a man living in Guatemala who happened to have the same name as one of the founding fathers of the United States—George C. Washington. The story goes that one day while Washington was waiting for his wife to join him for coffee, he noticed a dark, powdery substance forming on the spout of his silver coffeepot. As a chemist and inventor, he couldn't help but be curious. In 1906, after experimenting further, Washington began selling his instant coffee under the name Red E Coffee.

During World War I, the U.S. Army was Washington's number-one client, and his company provided soldiers with what became known as their "cup of George." His company dominated the coffee market for several decades.

Instant coffee once again became popular among American soldiers during World War II—Nescafé came steaming onto the market in 1938 and is still the world's leading instant coffee brand.

The instant beverage was updated in 1963 when Kraft introduced its Maxwell House freeze-dried instant coffee, which the company claimed tasted more similar to fresh-brewed coffee than any other instant coffee product. Within a few years, all major manufacturers had freeze-dried coffee products on the market.

Just Add Hot Water

In February 2009, Starbucks began serving instant coffee in single-serving packets. Long considered to be the dregs of the coffee world, instant coffee had always played second fiddle to its bigger brothers, espresso and freshly brewed coffee, but actually, Starbucks had been working on developing its instant coffee for more than 20 long years.

Don Valencia is credited with introducing instant coffee to Starbucks in the late 1980s. Valencia was the CEO of a biomedical firm where he used freeze-drying equipment to make instant coffee for backpacking trips and for Christmas gifts. He and his wife, Heather, brought a sample of the instant coffee into the Starbucks store in Pike Place Market, and it was eventually passed along to CEO Howard Schultz. Valencia was eventually hired to run Starbucks' research and development team. The new instant coffee product is called "Via," a play on Valencia's name.

Kaffia
in Basque (Spain)

STARBUCKS: TOTAL WORLD DOMINATION

They took away smoking, they took away drugs and promiscuous sex, they took away eating red meat and cat calling hot chicks on the street. All I have left is overpriced coffee, and by God I'm going to drink it!

–Brent Sienna, comedian

Familiar the World Over

I still remember the best cup of coffee I ever had. It wasn't in Mexico or France or even Guatemala; it was in Seoul, Korea, at the country's one and only Starbucks. What made it so memorable was a combination of the unbearable heat and humidity and the feeling that we were lost trekkers in an *Indiana Jones* movie—seeing that familiar green circle and mermaid was like seeing a mirage in the desert. Looking and feeling like Courtney Love on a bad day in rehab, I gasped and squealed with delight and relief at the thought of a cold, iced frappuccino. Up until that very moment, I had treated Starbucks's obnoxious cup-sizing names with derision and contempt and would not normally have been caught dead darkening the door of a Starbucks; but suddenly, a caramel frappuccino seemed like the answer to the very meaning of life.

Recognizing a familiar institution in a country halfway around the world—which, incidentally, sold warmed scarab beetles as a curbside snack—made me feel like I had died and gone to heaven that day. That's how they get you, you see—total world domination.

Shortly afterwards, Starbucks became totally integrated into the fabric of my life. Reminding me of my favorite lines from *So I Married an Axe Murderer*, I had always thought that Starbucks must put an addictive chemical in their coffee that makes you crave it fortnightly. I was snapped out of that misconception after a visit to a fair trade coffee cooperative in Guatemala, but for two or three years, Starbucks had me by the baristas.

Love it or hate it, Starbucks is here to stay. More than 40 million customers a week are served in its more than 13,000 stores. Many people believe that the proliferation of Starbucks marks the beginning of the end of the universe, or that it represents the decline of civilization. Others feel that Starbucks simply symbolizes the homogenization of the world, while some just like to treat themselves to familiar surroundings.

No matter your personal opinions, there is one thing that can't be doubted: Starbucks has left an indelible imprint on the entire planet. Like London's coffee houses and the cafés of Paris, Starbucks has had an undeniable impact on the social makeup of our world. It's a place for folk to get together, socialize, gossip, discuss ideas or simply unwind. If the words "venti-five-shot-sugarfree-vanilla-lactaid-light-foam-caramel-macchiato" make you cringe, do read on.

The average person who buys coffee outside the office to drink at work will spend the equivalent of a cross-country round-trip plane ticket every year.

In the Beginning

The men behind the most ubiquitous coffee chain in the world—English teacher Jerry Baldwin, history teacher Zev Siegl and writer Gordon Bowker—are the most unlikely trio ever to open a coffee shop and become big-business tycoons. And indeed, Baldwin and Siegel have admitted that they were just looking for "something to do." All three were in it for the adventure

more than the money and, ironically, claimed that they wanted to be "as far away as possible from the business world."

Bowker, the writer, loved coffee, and there was no quality coffee available anywhere in Seattle at the time, so he would drive across the border to a Vancouver roaster to get his beans. Eventually, the trio was carting so much coffee back from Canada that opening their own store seemed like a logical next step. Coffee was once again being smuggled across borders and, though he hardly had illegal seeds strapped to his midsection, Bowker was essentially a modern-day Baba Budan.

The First Starbucks

The original Starbucks opened its doors in March 1971 at 2000 Western Avenue in Seattle, Washington. It was *not* in the Pike Place Market nor in the Arcade as many people think, but just north, across the street from the public market.

This misconception exists because the first Starbucks wasn't even really a Starbucks at all. The first retail Starbucks coffee drink concept store was originally called Il Giornale and was located on 4th Avenue in downtown Seattle. There was only ever one of these stores, and it was started by an ambitious Starbucks employee named Howard Schultz.

But we'll get to that soon.

The Bean Scene

Starbucks began by selling beans for customers to take home. Peet's Coffee and Tea House, which had been open since 1966, supplied them with the coffee beans. Starbucks and Peet's are considered to be industry trailblazers of the '60s and '70s.

In 1976, five years after opening, Starbucks changed locations and moved to Seattle's Pike Place Market, where it still stands today. Since the market is designated as a historic monument, the chain's oldest store retains its original look.

Entrepreneur Howard Schultz joined the company in 1982 as the director of marketing. He was competitive, crazy about coffee and an aggressive and bold businessman. On a trip to Milan, Italy, Schultz saw the revenue potential that could be generated from creating customers who would come in to purchase coffee daily instead of weekly. He wanted to start selling coffee and espresso drinks as well as beans. The owners initially rejected this idea, believing that getting into the beverage business would distract the company from its primary focus—to them, coffee was something to be prepared at home.

The Name

The Starbucks chain took its name from a character in Herman Melville's novel *Moby Dick*.

The name also conveniently brings up the idea of stardom and big bucks—both very appealing to the typical American consumer. As author Taylor Clark points out, the word manages to evoke the vaguely mystical, hints at an antique tradition and subtly reminds customers what they're there to spend.

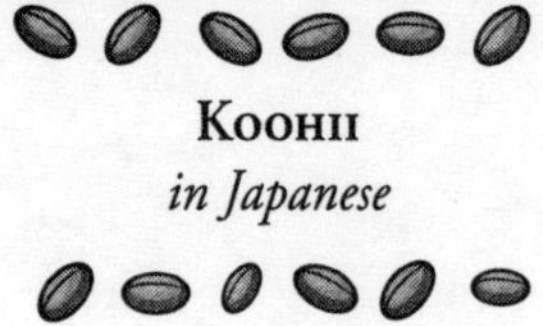

Koohii
in Japanese

SIRENS, MERMAIDS AND SPLIT-TAILS, OH MY!

Lurid Logos

Have you ever found yourself questioning the Starbucks logo? No? Well, you might be one of the few. Last year, Starbucks stores in the U.S. went retro, returning to their '80s logo, which was a brown, bare-chested, split-tailed mermaid.

Say what?

Yep. The original Starbucks logo was a naughty siren chillin' with her tail out of the water. And the Starbucks mermaid has been a source of much controversy for most of the 30 years that she has been around.

Starbucks had to change their corporate logo because, shockingly, some consumers found the topless siren too lurid and sexually suggestive. They found it, shall we say, tough to swallow with their morning coffee.

A simplified logo was introduced in 1987, hiding the siren's breasts under waves of hair. Interpretations abounded! She has giant pineapples for tail legs! She's doing a difficult yoga pose! She's a contortionist in Cirque du Soleil!

Successful product branding, especially to a large population of disparate people, requires a logo that is completely innocuous, so Starbucks again decided to play it safe—the image was cropped and enlarged so the split in the siren's tail and her scandalous belly button would no longer show. The only indication now that the female icon is still a sea creature is the wavy lines. The logo is so ambiguous and squeaky clean that you can't even tell what she is holding anymore. Two scaly fish? Oven mitts? Dumbbells?

Mermaid Swimming in Controversy

When Starbucks brought back the original logo in 2008 for a limited time, you can just imagine the controversy and how upset it made some communities.

One Christian group boycotted Starbucks altogether. "The Starbucks logo has a naked woman on it with her legs spread like a prostitute," explained Mark Dice, founder of the group. "Need I say more? It's extremely poor taste, and the company might as well call themselves Slutbucks."

That's a bit of a leap, but so are some other comments, which have included consternation regarding the mermaid's size, especially from women. Surprisingly, she has in fact been called "The Chubby Mermaid." Has society has been so brainwashed and conditioned by Ariel, the "little" mermaid, that the Starbucks siren is now our designated Fat Chick?

Crowning Glory

In Jerusalem, in March 2009, an Egyptian religious leader made what is quite possibly the most ludicrous and perplexing complaint against Starbucks ever. He called for a boycott against Starbucks throughout the entire Arab world, claiming that the mermaid is actually Queen Esther. Queen who? Queen Esther is the queen of the Jews. In what can only be described as a questionable interpretation, the cleric claimed that the crown on the mermaid's head was the crown of the Persian kingdom, and then he made the rather puzzling leap based on this "fact" alone that the coffee shop should be boycotted by all Arabs, on principle.

Pass the Sugar

I know what you're thinking: what does all this have to do with coffee? Mermaids, sirens—what's the difference? And why did Starbucks choose one to be their mascot in the first place? Well, according to the ancient Greeks, sirens and mermaids were in the business of seducing mariners with songs and promises of sex, and then killing them when they came near.

Um…okay? That still doesn't explain why a mermaid-siren is Starbucks' icon. Author Heinz Insu Fenkl believes that "the original logo made quite explicit that Starbucks was using the lure of female sexuality to draw the customer to their coffee, but now you can see that the coffee is linked to the double lure of ultimate wisdom and the pleasures of the flesh."

If you ask Doug Fast, the logo's designer, he simply says that the woman depicted is based on a Greek mythological siren-half-woman-half-fish. You get the distinct impression that he just thought it would look *cool*—you know, back in 1971 when he designed it for a little independent Seattle coffee shop.

Il Giornale

But actually, the logo was a combination of two logos from two different businesses. Howard Schultz, frustrated that he couldn't convince the Starbucks owners to start serving espresso, opened his own espresso café in 1986 called Il Giornale. Il Giornale literally means "the newspaper," though the name was intended to suggest something that was consumed on a daily basis. Schultz was confident that there was big money to be made selling premade drinks.

A year later, Baldwin and Bowker were ready to sell their business, and Schultz jumped at the chance to buy Starbucks and remake it into the espresso bar concept he had just begun at Il Giornale.

In Howard Schultz's autobiography, *Pour Your Heart into It*, he explains that the "early siren, bare breasted and Rubenesque, was supposed to be as seductive as coffee itself." See, she's *Rubenesque*, not "chubby."

So there you have it—the next time you lift a cup of Starbucks coffee to your lips, make sure to take a moment to be seduced by the sultry siren on your cup. And for those of you scoffing at this concept, it's hard to argue against the fact that all of North America—and the world, for that matter—has already been seduced by this sexy coffee.

DID YOU KNOW?

Employees and those who are extremely familiar with Starbucks write SBUX, which is its Dow Jones trading name.

THE THIRD PLACE

Feeling Right at Home

Do you go to Starbucks so often that it feels like a second home? Well, that's good. It's exactly what the company is banking on—and it's no accident.

The concept was originally developed by urban sociologist Ray Oldenburg, who argues that coffee shops, like pubs in England and cafés in France, offer a "third place" between home and work where camaraderie can be built and conversations can flourish.

Indeed, in the '90s TV sitcom *Cheers*, one of the series' foundations was to make patrons feel at home. It was the "third place" where "everybody knows your name."

Oldenburg even goes so far as to suggest that society is damaged by the omission of third-place environments from many present-day suburbs and cities. This "third place" premise is a concept that Starbucks latched onto and ran with.

So Why All the Fuss?

Ever wonder how they did it? How did Starbucks manage to take two things that are neither original nor exclusive—coffee and milk—and charge so much for it? How did coffee—a drink that people can buy anywhere, anytime and much cheaper—get catapulted to such great heights? Well, for one, Starbucks is the master at creating brand loyalty, and they successfully managed to make customers believe that *their* coffee is the best and that no other coffee will do. And part of that has a lot to do with how they name their coffee.

The Skinny on Starbucks Names

Ever wonder what happened to the plain-old medium coffee? What's in a Starbucks coffee name, anyway? Starbucks' coffee lingo likely originated from Italian coffee bars around the world, most of which have a long heritage of having specific names for different types of coffee. But Starbucks seems to have overcomplicated matters by separating the size, strength, sweetness, flavor, milk, temperature, level of froth and calories of the beverage. For example, a "cappuccino with less foam and no chocolate" should actually be called a "flat white." And a "no-foam latte to go" should actually be called a "wet latte with wings."

So why is this? Well, the company created overly elaborate names for their coffee to give consumers a sense of belonging, an attitude of elitism and to add cachet to their product. Coffee became chic, a trend that oozed cool and represented hipness.

The Younger, the Better

As you can imagine, this had great appeal for teenage girls, who quickly latched onto this symbol of maturity that had a celebrity-endorsed coolness about it. The target group for Starbucks is also

14- to 25-year-olds and—as any company will tell you—it is ideal for consumers to become hooked from a very young age.

Coffee Craze

In 1995, coffee went *splat!* into the American marketplace. Everyone was crazy about caffeine—caffeinated lipstick called "lipachino," caffeinated soap and, yes, even coffee pantyhose were available. Reportedly, the "Coffee Tights" eliminated cellulite by activating skin cells with caffeine microcapsules that were laced into the fabric's fibers.

Shiny Happy People Consuming Expensive Milk Products

"Coffee drinks" of today are overwhelmingly dominated by milk—even with a standard two shots of espresso, a grande or venti beverage has seven to eight times as much milk as coffee. Coffee makes up only five to ten percent of the drink, and the rest is milk and sugar. These drinks are not coffee drinks flavored with hot milk as much as they are milk drinks flavored with coffee.

> *Consumers are always ordering mutant beverages [...] that must be made one at a time via a lengthy and complex process involving approximately one coffee bean, three quarts of dairy products and what appears to be a small nuclear reactor.*
>
> –Dave Barry, columnist

Milk was rarely added to coffee before the 19th century since fresh milk was too unstable and dangerous to drink before pasteurization and refrigeration became commonplace in 1865. Coffee with milk was made by boiling the milk with the coffee grounds, a preparation mainly intended for invalids, who were considered second-class citizens.

Mocha Choca Latté Ya Ya

Starbucks offers 87,000 different variations of the average cup of joe. Technically, a "venti-wet-cappuccino-extra-hot" and a "tall-double-190-degree-no-foam-latte" are the same drink, but the point is that Starbucks not only caters to, but *celebrates* your finicky order. According to Taylor Clark, part of the reason that Starbucks has been so successful is because they glorify and indulge our neurotic tendencies.

Everyone knows nowadays that when you order a drink at Starbucks, the cashier will write the order on the side of the cup with a felt pen. But in the early Starbucks days, when an employee took a customer's order, the desired drink would be indicated to the barista based on a specific cup position. An upside-down cup with the logo facing forward and slightly to the left, for example would mean the customer had ordered a "skim-milk-decaf-cappuccino."

Starbucks Real Estate

In 1989, there were a grand total of 585 coffee houses in the United States. In 2007, there were approximately 24,000 and counting. Starbucks played a large part in that—its real estate development division has more employees than the average coffee company has in total. Since it couldn't have a monopoly on coffee, which is widely available everywhere, Starbucks focused on controlling the real estate.

Similar to the McDonald's model, Starbucks has made itself into an unavoidable obstacle in people's daily paths. Here's how:

When deciding on a location, Starbucks targets high-income, high-education areas first because better-educated people usually have more disposable income and are more inclined to patronize their stores.

 Almost every Starbucks you pass on your way into the downtown core will be on your right-hand side because morning commuters are more likely to stop if they don't have to attempt a left-hand turn in rush-hour traffic.

 Starbucks positions stores near dry cleaners and video rental shops to give customers two opportunities to buy coffee: once when dropping something off, and again when picking it up.

 The company has been known to pay rent on retail space just to keep it empty.

 Starbucks keeps a continual eye on corner lots and buys them as soon as they become available. Intersections are considered ideal sites for coffee shops because they are high-visibility locations.

The chain does not franchise its outlets, which is why it has no qualms about opening stores across the street from one another. It doesn't have to worry about franchisees clamoring about the decrease in sales. This particular brand of cannibalism saturates the market and makes their stores not only more convenient, but virtually impossible to avoid.

DID YOU KNOW?

People who buy coffee primarily at drive-through windows on their way to work will spend as many as 45 hours a year waiting in line.

It's a Miracle!

Starbucks is even powerful enough to turn sinners into churchgoers. When one Southern Baptist pastor in Cooper City, Florida, set out to boost attendance at his church's 2006 Easter service, he sent word promising a $10 Starbucks gift card to every new parishioner.

The Miami Herald reported that on Easter Sunday, almost double the church's normal Easter attendance—about 8500 people—showed up to claim their prize. The church actually had to turn people away at the parking lot. Apparently, the path to salvation includes a no-foam-extra-hot-double-tall-vanilla-soy-latte.

There is a Texas man who calls himself Winter who has made it his life's mission since 1997 to visit every Starbucks store on the planet. He has made it to 8444 locations in the U.S. so far—or approximately 98.9 percent—and another 664 stores in Canada, Britain, Spain, France, Japan, Mexico, Hong Kong, Puerto Rico, Ireland, Switzerland, Germany, Austria , Greece, Jordan, Lebanon and Turkey. The most stores he has hit in one day is 27. Track his progress by visiting www.starbuckseverywhere.net.

FAST STARBUCKS FACTS

Eight Things You Probably Didn't Know About Starbucks

- Starbucks Coffee, Tea and Spice stopped carrying spices in 1989 after a few cats overdosed on their catnip.
- Some estimates place the total cost for a cup of Starbucks coffee—including materials, staff and service—at less than 50 cents a cup. Since they charge anywhere between $3 and $4 for their product, this gives the retailer a profit margin of more than 80 percent. Some estimates have gone as low as six cents per cup if you only count the cost of the coffee itself.
- Starbucks has influenced automatic traffic patterns. According to the U.S. Department of Transportation, the number of short stops made by morning commuters went up nearly 400 percent between 1995 and 2001, leading to greater fuel waste, higher pollution and worse gridlock as more drivers pull on and off the road. Not surprisingly, this has been dubbed "the Starbucks Effect."
- Starbucks paid a firm to hypnotize its customers. What they discovered was that consumers really wanted an "emotional" connection with their coffee.
- There are Starbucks stores located in all the following unlikely places: Guantanamo Bay Naval Base in Cuba; a Christian church in Munster, Indiana; Beirut, Lebanon; and the Great Wall of China. Surprisingly, however, there isn't one to be found within 40 miles of the town of Starbuck, Washington—or at least there wasn't at the time of print.

- On average, Starbucks has opened more than 2000 coffee houses per year—an average of six new stores per day. The company plans to surpass 20,000 stores in the U.S. alone and 40,000 stores overall, which would make it the biggest chain on the planet. Some see the ubiquity as the height of convenience; others take it as a sign of the impending apocalypse.

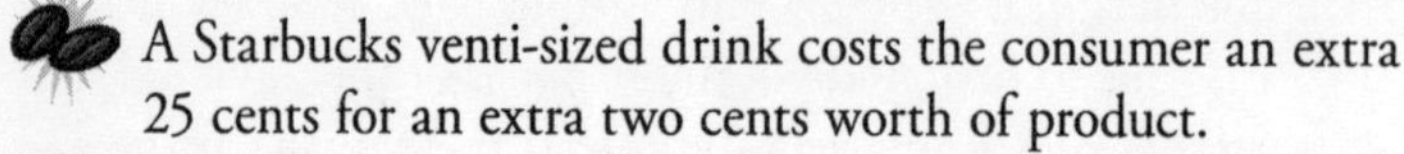

- A Starbucks venti-sized drink costs the consumer an extra 25 cents for an extra two cents worth of product.

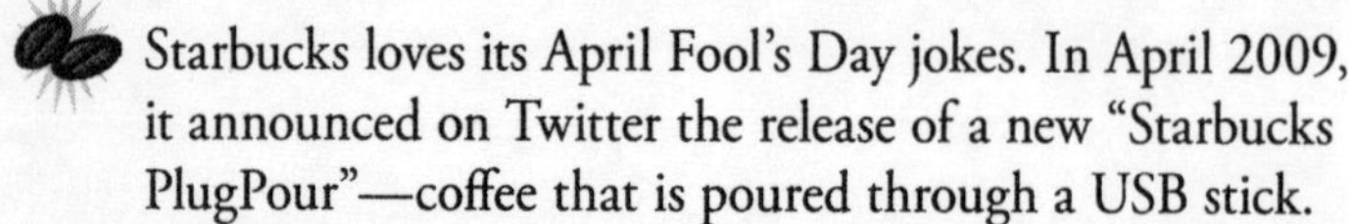

- Starbucks loves its April Fool's Day jokes. In April 2009, it announced on Twitter the release of a new "Starbucks PlugPour"—coffee that is poured through a USB stick.

The Starbucks Way

- Starbucks roasts at four plants in the United States and Amsterdam. It is the darkest of all the roasters in the U.S.
- Opened bags of beans are discarded after one week. Although it may be wasteful, it does attest to the quality of the coffee you are drinking.
- Hot coffee is stored in thermal carafes and not on burners, making for a better-flavored cup.
- Starbucks uses two tablespoons of ground coffee for each six ounces of water, which is double the more standard recipe of one tablespoon per six ounces of water.
- The company's service target is three minutes from when the customer walks in the door to when the beverage is served.
- Starbucks uses automated espresso machines that grind, tamp and pull espresso shots in the push of a button to save service time. The steam wand is also programmed to stop at exactly the right temperature.
- On November 4, 2008, in order to increase voter turnout for the presidential elections, Starbucks offered a free tall cup of coffee to all registered voters.

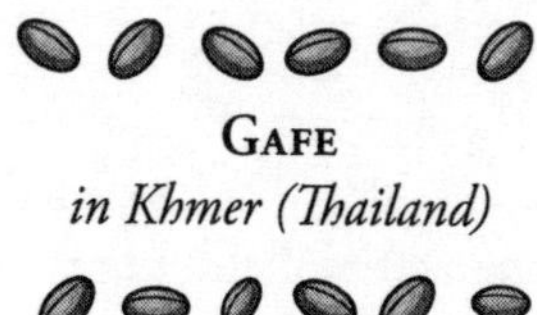

THE STORY OF TIM HORTONS

Everyone knows that a double-double-from-Tim-Hortons kind of guy wouldn't be caught dead ordering a venti-soy-latte from Starbucks.

–Steve Maich, *Maclean's* magazine columnist

Timmies

These days, Tim Hortons is considered an iconic and quintessentially Canadian company. "Timmies" is Canada's largest coffee and baked goods chain, with more than 2900 stores in Canada and over 500 locations in the United States. Everyone reading this has no doubt had a double-double on a long and seemingly never-ending road trip or has brought a pack of Timbits to share at a staff meeting, hockey game or garage sale. But how many people know the history behind its namesake? And how many Canadians realize that this country's signature brand name has since 1995 actually been an American-owned company?

Tim Horton on Ice

Tim Horton was a defenseman for the Toronto Maple Leafs and, later, the Buffalo Sabres. He was a strong player, selected for six All-Star teams, and he lasted an impressive 24 seasons in the NHL. He won four Stanley Cups, and many believe that Tim Horton invented the slap shot. But for the average Canadian, he isn't remembered for anything that happened on the ice; rather, he is known for his iced caps, coffee and tasty baked goods.

It's odd when you think about it—hockey is a Canadian institution, a way of life. So when someone who played professional hockey for 22 years is *more famous* for doing something else, it's a bit of a paradox.

Tim Horton's birth name was actually Miles Gilbert. He was named after one of his grandfathers following the family tradition, but his mother had always wanted to name him Tim and started calling him that as soon as he was born.

No Play, No Pay

After a serious on-ice injury in which he broke his leg and his jawbone, Horton began searching for other sources of income, all too aware that his hockey career had a shelf life. Hockey players were treated very differently in the 1950s and 1960s—they did not hold the same revered status that many players enjoy today. In fact, like most players of his era, Horton was treated with contempt by his employer and, though it's hard to believe now, he was forced to take summer jobs to make ends meet. After having missed much of the 1955 season because of an injury, Horton had a difficult time trying to support his wife and four young children and the family nearly went broke.

Pass the Dutchie

After an unsuccessful attempt to open a chain of hamburger stands, Horton and his friend Jim Charade starting talking about coffee and doughnuts. But first they needed financial help, so Horton ran an ad in the local newspaper that was answered by Ron Joyce, a Hamilton police officer. Joyce invested $10,000 in the store and developed an initial business plan that aimed at opening 10 stores.

The first Tim Hortons store opened in Hamilton in 1964. Horton personally created the Dutchie and Apple Fritter, which have been the long-standing champions in the Canadian doughnut world and continue to be two of the most popular doughnuts today.

In 1974, Horton died in a car accident on his way home to Buffalo. He had just played a game in Toronto, and it was discovered that he had not only consumed alcohol but was taking painkillers for a sore jaw. He was 44 years old.

In the years since his death, friends and family have revealed that Tim Horton drank too much, that he and his wife endured a difficult and sometimes fractious marriage, and that he struggled to reconcile his pro-hockey lifestyle with his family life. Horton was inducted into the Hockey Hall of Fame in 1977.

According to freelance hockey journalist Joe Pelletier, Tim Horton, along with his hockey-playing contemporaries, served to bridge hockey's ancient and modern histories: "He saw the debut of *Hockey Night in Canada*, the rise of the hockey card and the move from black-and-white to color television. His salary rose from $9000 to $150,000. He played with Max Bentley and against Dennis Potvin. He witnessed the NHL's expansion from the cozy Original Six to 14 teams. The league Horton joined was a cottage industry. By the time he played his last game in 1974, the NHL was in the midst of its first shaky attempts to become a lucrative entertainment conglomerate."

A year after his death, Horton's widow sold the family's share of the store to Ron Joyce for $1 million dollars and a Cadillac Eldorado. Lori Horton lived to regret this controversial transaction and tried unsuccessfully to overturn it, so that, though the chain continues to bear the name, none of the wealth actually belongs to the Horton family.

Ron Joyce remained the sole owner of Tim Hortons until he merged the chain with Wendy's in 1995. At the time of Tim's death, there were only 40 Tim Hortons stores; as of March 2009, there are over 3400 restaurants systemwide, with 2930 in Canada and 527 in the United States. Tim Hortons rings up over $1 billion in sales every year, with revenue exceeding $400 million annually.

Cop Cups

Where do all the jokes about cops and doughnut shops come from? Well, the truth is that franchises generally offer free coffee and doughnuts to any police officer in uniform. This is meant as a gesture of good will, as well as being a simple way to increase police presence in the area.

Stolen Glory

In 2002, a 1967 Stanley Cup ring appeared for auction in Toronto auction house. The ring had been stolen from Horton's wife, Lori, in 1998. Police seized it and returned it to the grateful widow, who died not long after its return, several years after losing a long legal battle to retain an interest in the company her husband founded.

The movie *Wayne's World* includes a stop at "Stan Mikita's Doughnuts." Stan Mikita is a Canadian-born hockey player who led the Chicago Blackhawks to a Stanley Cup victory in 1961. This is *Wayne's World* creator Mike Myers taking a good-hearted, albeit obvious, poke at Canada's favorite coffee and doughnut chain.

Rrroll Up the Rim

"Rrroll up the Rim to win!" time at Tim Hortons is practically considered a holiday season in Canada. February marks this special time when customers get the chance to win prizes, most of which are coffee and doughnuts, and we've been Rrrolling up the Rim for 23 years now. Let's face it—it's pretty much up there with the Stanley Cup as far as great Canadian traditions go.

The Timbits King

Although very few people may actually know who he is, Ron Joyce is the man behind the brand: Tim Hortons co-founder and business mogul. Now almost 80, he is worth more than an estimated $1.1 billion. Joyce's story of hard luck and entrepreneurial spirit could be ripped right from the pages of a made-for-TV movie. From his humble beginnings in Tatamagouche, Nova Scotia, no one could ever have predicted that he would become one of the richest men in Canada.

Joyce's tradesman father died when he was three, leaving a widow to raise three children on welfare. Joyce left school in grade nine and moved to Ontario, taking jobs as a factory worker or in tobacco fields before eventually becoming a sailor. After five years in the navy, he became a police officer. He joined forces with Horton two years later, in 1965, becoming a full partner in the business in 1967.

Joyce spent the next 30 years building his empire and, by 1995, Tim Hortons had opened 1000 outlets. Joyce has seven children, but none of them seemed interested in taking over the company. When he was 65, Joyce negotiated a deal with the Wendy's International Inc. hamburger chain in the U.S. and, in return for relinquishing control, Joyce was rewarded $16.5 million in Wendy's shares. In a delicious example of poetic justice, Joyce's son, Ron Jr., married Tim Horton's daughter, Jeri-Lyn, reuniting the Horton family with the company founded upon their name.

In more recent news, it was announced on Tim Hortons' website in June 2009 that the company would no longer be owned by Wendy's and, pending a stockholders meeting in September 2009, is set to become a stand-alone Canadian public company trading on the Toronto Stock Exchange and the New York Stock Exchange under the name "New THI (Tim Hortons Inc.)," with its corporate head office in Oakville, Ontario, Canada.

TIMMIES OVERSEAS

Serving the Troops in Kandahar

In November 2006, the Canadian government spent $1.5 million to build a Tim Hortons in Kandahar for the troops stationed there. Tim Hortons waived their $450,000 franchise fee and all other expenses were paid for by Canadian taxpayers.

If U.S. soldiers serving in the Kandahar base could have their own Burger King, Subway and Pizza Hut franchises then, with thousands of Canadian troops stationed in southern Afghanistan, senior Canadian officers decided it just wouldn't really be a Canadian base without a Timmies.

The store serves Timbits and double-doubles to the approximately 2200 Canadian Forces members and 5000 personnel from other countries. Believe it or not, 1300 customers per day file through the Kandahar Tim Hortons from 12 different countries stationed on the base.

Personnel pay prices comparable to those in Canada, and profits from this project are reinvested in morale and welfare programs for Canadian Forces members. The government expected to recoup their expenses within four or five years, and most Canadians felt this was a small price to pay to give troops a little taste of home.

Picking Up the Lingo

Do you speak Tim Hortonese? Ordering a regular coffee in Tim Hortons language will get you one milk and one sugar. Whereas Canadian soldiers file in and out as if they were on a conveyor belt, for some of the troops on the Kandahar Base, the double-double and Timbit lingo has taken some getting used to. And FYI: a Dutchie is a type of doughnut, not a drug reference.

Coffee by Nationality

Some of the employees at Tim Hortons Kandahar boast that they can tell a soldier's nationality at the base even if they speak perfect English and are not wearing a uniform, simply by what they order.

Apparently, the British and the Dutch mostly order Boston creams and Canadian maples, and the Americans are more likely to order five dozen doughnuts at a time. The British and the Dutch also always order very sweet cappuccinos. And what do the Canadians order? Why, bagels and coffee, of course.

Fran-glazed Doughnuts

According to the staff, the most humorous thing that happens at the Tim Hortons in Kandahar involves Canada's southern neighbors. Canada, being a bilingual country, requires that all menu signage must contain both English and French names. Some of the American troops sometimes come up and ask for an "apple-fritter-beignes-aux-pommes" or an "iced-cap-glacé."

It's an honest mistake, *n'est-ce pas*?

SECOND CUP

The Second Cup Success Story

Second Cup is a leading specialty coffee company in Canada with approximately 400 franchised cafés across the country.

The company's founder, Frank O'Dea, also has a story of the made-for-TV variety. Before founding Second Cup, you see, Frank O'Dea was homeless. In his teens and early twenties, he was living in 50-cent-a-night flophouses in Toronto, where just surviving was about all one could do in a day.

At 23, Frank began to pull himself out of that life and rejoined society. Within a few short years, he co-founded Second Cup, which soon became the largest chain of gourmet coffees and teas in Canada. O'Dea claims that he is the one to have come up with the idea of coffee as a treat. He started charging more and marketing it to consumers as a way to reward themselves for all their hard work.

He sold the chain to Mmmuffins founder Michael Bregman in 1988 and went on to co-found Proshred Security, a company that pioneered the entire industry of on-site confidential document destruction.

Today, O'Dea is a motivational speaker and travels the country telling his story of how he went from homelessness to entrepreneurship. Check him out at www.frankodea.com.

FAST-FOOD COFFEE

Coffee has two virtues: it is wet and it is warm.

–Dutch saying

Would You Like Fries With That?

These days, everyone wants to get a sip of the high-end coffee craze that has been sweeping the world. If you told people 10 years ago that they would be buying gourmet coffee at McDonald's, they likely would have McLaughed in your face.

The fast-food chains are cashing in on America's love affair with quality java and are now starting to feature their very own frothy coffee drinks. In 2005, McDonald's also started offering organic coffee roasted by Green Mountain Coffee Roasters at 650 locations in New England and Albany, New York.

McCafé

But long before then, McDonald's had already opened a Starbucks-style coffee bar that they called McCafé. No joke. Reports indicated that McCafé outlets, which featured lattes, espressos and the like, generated 15 percent more revenue than a regular McDonald's and, by 2003, McCafé was the largest coffee shop brand in Australia and New Zealand. Since then, McDonald's has expanded to Japan and other countries, and there are currently 1300 McCafés worldwide, with the expectation of having the majority of its 14,000 U.S. stores converted by mid-2009.

Burger King, not to be left behind, now lets you order coffee brewed one cup at a time so you avoid that burned taste. Dunkin' Donuts, which has been offering specialty brews for years, claims to have sold nearly a billion cups of coffee in 2005, more than any other retailer in the country.

Slam Dunkin'

In 2007, Dunkin' Donuts surprised everyone by edging out Starbucks for first place as the hottest coffee chain: for the first time since 2002, Starbucks had some real competition. In a national taste test held in 10 major U.S. cities, coffee drinkers chose Dunkin' Donuts coffee over Starbucks 58 percent of the time. The survey was even conducted in Starbucks-preferred territories such as Seattle and Los Angeles.

Dunkin' Donuts has previously proven that it is not afraid to get "dough" and dirty. In the early 2000s, it successfully managed to beat out Krispy Kreme as the number one doughnut chain. Experts believe—especially in the current economy—that consumers prefer a cheaper way of getting their high-end java fix.

CORPORATE COFFEE CASES

Lawsuits are nothing new for big corporations or coffee companies. They pretty much come with the territory. Here are just a few examples of court cases involving coffee giants, including Starbucks, McDonald's and Tim Hortons. These cases are some of the biggest and most well known—they have taken as many as 15 years to resolve, clogging up the courts and costing hundreds of thousands of dollars.

The McDonald's Coffee Lawsuit

The McDonald's Coffee Case has been referred to as everything from frivolous and ludicrous to legitimate and misunderstood. Everyone knows or has heard about it, and to this day, 17 years after it started, it is still one of the best-known and most controversial lawsuits of all time.

Everyone seems to have an opinion of this highly publicized case. Many people remain extremely unsympathetic, stating that the plaintiff ordered hot coffee, received hot coffee and then sued McDonald's because it was hot. Others feel that the plaintiff had a legitimate case and argue that McDonald's was deliberately being negligent. On one thing everyone is in agreement: it was a complex and definitive learning experience for lawyers, consumers and corporations alike. For many, it continues to represent the base problems of the civil justice system.

Gather 'round—this is a tale of terrible injury, corporate indifference, personal greed and millions of dollars.

Background

On February 27, 1992, in Albuquerque, New Mexico, 79-year-old Stella Liebeck went through a McDonald's drive-through with her grandson, Chris. She was riding in the passenger seat of her Ford Probe and ordered an eight-ounce cup of coffee.

Some accounts state that they parked the car so she could add cream and sugar, while others state that she tried to open the lid while the car was still moving. In either case, Liebeck put the cup between her knees and pulled the lid too vigorously, spilling hot coffee all over herself.

Reportedly, it took about 90 seconds before she was able to remove her pants, at which point the coffee had already scalded her thighs, buttocks and groin.

Liebeck was rushed to a hospital where doctors diagnosed her with third-degree burns on six percent of her body and lesser burns on an additional 16 percent of her body. In total, nearly a quarter

of her skin had been burned in the accident. Liebeck remained hospitalized for eight days while she underwent skin-graft surgery; she also endured two years of follow-up treatment.

Don't Cry Over Spilled Coffee

In 1993, Liebeck asked McDonald's for $20,000 to cover her medical bills, blaming the company and its coffee for her injuries. McDonald's made a counteroffer: $800. Liebeck, a former department store clerk, had never filed a lawsuit before and had no intention of doing so until McDonald's so flatly turned her down.

Feeling she had no other choice, Liebeck hired attorney Reed Morgan and sued McDonald's for $90,000, accusing the company of "gross negligence" for selling "unreasonably dangerous" and "defectively manufactured" coffee. McDonald's, though, still wouldn't settle.

Too Haughty to Handle

And why not? It would seem that a multibillion-dollar corporation would want to pay out a small amount to make the lawsuit—and the bad publicity—go away. But here's the thing: McDonald's had known for years that their coffee was served much hotter than the coffee at other restaurants. It was *intentionally* hotter—by at least 20°F—because, according to McDonald's, most drive-through customers were travelers and commuters who wanted their coffee to remain hotter for a longer time.

Not only that, McDonald's also knew that sometimes the temperature of its coffee had caused scalding. In the 10 years preceding Liebeck's lawsuit, the company had received more than 700 complaints about the temperature of its coffee. Every case had been thrown out of court for being frivolous—clearly, McDonald's thought this suit would be no different from all the others. And indeed, 12 courts threw the case out before it finally went to trial in New Mexico.

The Great Debate

Those 700 complaints were used to argue that McDonald's had consistently sold dangerously hot coffee and "didn't care" about its customers. A McDonald's quality assurance manager testified that the corporation was aware of the risk of serving dangerously hot coffee but had no plans to either turn down the heat or to post warning labels about the possibility of severe burns.

The rate of complaints amounted to one in 24 million cups of coffee sold, which McDonald's didn't feel was enough to necessitate a chain-wide change. To put this in perspective, in a given year one in four million Americans will be killed by lightning, and another one in 20 million will drown in a five-gallon bucket of water.

How Hot Was the Coffee?

McDonald's required their coffee to be served at between 180 to 190°F (water boils at 212°F). At 180°F, coffee can cause a third-degree burn in only two seconds of contact. Most other fast-food chains served their coffee at 140°F. However, one misconception about the coffee case is that there was no warning label on the cup. Actually, there was! But the jury felt that the warning label was too small and not cautionary enough.

The Verdict

According to *The Wall Street Journal*, it was McDonald's callousness that was the issue, and even jurors who thought the suit had been blown out of proportion were overwhelmed by the evidence against the corporation. The jury found McDonald's was 80 percent responsible for serving coffee it knew could cause burns without a decently sized warning label, and Liebeck was held 20 percent accountable for spilling the cup.

A punitive amount of $2.7 million was awarded to Liebeck, with an additional $160,000 for compensatory damages. That might seem like a lot of money, but keep in mind that McDonald's generates revenues in excess of $1.3 million *daily* from the sale of coffee, selling one billion cups each year. The amount awarded to Liebeck was the equivalent of just two days of coffee sales.

The judge later reduced the punitive amount to $480,000. Both sides appealed the verdict, and the parties eventually settled at $600,000 in 1994, which was triple the amount that Liebeck had originally sued for.

The Last Drop

McDonald's also promised to reduce the temperature of its coffee to about 160°F, which it did. But since 1994, McDonald's admits it has slowly raised it back up to 180°F, the same temperature that gave a 79-year-old woman burns all over her lower body.

Today, Starbucks serves their coffee even hotter than McDonald's ever did. It seems to be a no-win argument either way. At what point does common sense come into play, and at what point are the big corporations being negligent?

No matter your position, the case is as "hotly" debated today as it ever was.

Never Too Hot, Never Too Cold

Since then, there have been a dizzying array of variations on the McDonald's hot coffee case. Coffee is too hot, lids are too tight, lids are not tight enough. Just one example: in February 2008, 77-year-old Rachel Moltner blew her lid after ordering a hot tea from a Starbucks in Manhattan. Having trouble removing the too-tight lid, Moltner spilled the burning-hot beverage all over herself. She underwent skin grafts for her second- and third-degree burns, and then broke her tailbone falling out of bed during her resulting five-week hospital stay. Moltner sued Starbucks for $3 million. The case is still pending as the parties haggle over federal jurisdiction.

Tim Hortons' Toonie Case

Hundreds of thousands of dollars in legal fees over a Canadian toonie? Not even working-class affection for Tim Hortons' brand of coffee can shield it from litigation. In 1999, a pregnant Tim Hortons employee was charged with stealing a toonie and other loose change by allegedly placing money that belonged to Tim Hortons into her personal tip jar. The employee was a single mother of four, and she claimed that she was just taking back a tip she had put into the till earlier in her shift.

The $7-an-hour employee was subsequently fired and then tried to sue Tim Hortons for wrongful dismissal. A jury dismissed her case in 2006, after which she turned to the Ontario Court of Appeal. Claiming that she was just trying to "clear her name," the Toronto employee sued for $10 million in damages, down from her original $23 million suit.

Tim Hortons allegedly had the theft on tape and released a statement that revenues at that store were lower by as much as $100 per shift when the employee in question was working. Tim Hortons finally won the case once and for all in May 2008, nine years after the incident took place.

Timbitgate

Another employee of a Tim Hortons franchise in London, Ontario, was also caught on surveillance video, giving away a 17-cent Timbit to appease a cranky 11-month-old. Two days later, the employee, a single mother, was called into the office by three store managers and promptly fired for theft.

When the story went public and the company realized what a public relations nightmare it could potentially become, a spokesperson for the company quickly apologized and told reporters that the managers who fired her were in the wrong and that the woman had been rehired and offered a similar job at another store.

Starbucks Toilet Bowl: 1, Tourist: 0

Most of us would probably assume that we're reasonably safe from harm in the bathroom. No harm can come to us in the can, right? Well, in 1999, a Canadian tourist named Edward Skwarek sued a New York Starbucks store after claiming that a faulty toilet seat had crushed a highly sensitive part of his anatomy against the toilet bowl, catching it between seat and bowl. According to *The Toronto Star*, this vicious attack by the assaulting seat left his man parts "bruised, crushed and rendered ineffective."

He sued the giant coffee retailer for $1.5 million. In the suit, he alleged that the coffee house was careless in "allowing a defective toilet seat to remain open…causing a hazardous and unsafe condition…in its public restrooms."

Skwarek sought $1 million in damages and his wife also sued for $500,000, seeing as she had been "deprived of his services." Personally, this author would like to meet the man whose "services" are worth half a million dollars. In truth, his wife was probably suing because the real damage is that she will never be able to get her husband to put the toilet seat down again.

Alan Gulick, a spokesman at Starbucks, said the company had "no comment."

No word on how the matter was resolved, but proud men everywhere are probably asking themselves if it would be worth a million dollars to have their name permanently associated with a news story like this.

Lack of Freedom in the Land of the Free?

One American resident, originally from Estonia, says she feels less free in the United States than she did in the former Soviet Union. She makes it a point to show her visiting friends a sight they could never see in the old country. They laugh, they point,

they whip out cameras and take pictures. Is it of the Everglades? No. Is it of Mount Rushmore or Lady Liberty? No.

They take pictures of all the idiot signs. These, she said, crack her friends up: "Caution: Coffee is hot." Apparently elsewhere in the world, you don't need a sign to know this!

Kafe
in Breton

DIFFERENT STROKES FOR DIFFERENT FOLKS

Everyone has their own way of doing it—drinking coffee, that is. The Italians drink their espresso with sugar; the Germans and Swiss with equal parts of hot chocolate; the Mexicans add cinnamon; the Belgians add chocolate; Moroccans drink their coffee with peppercorns; the Ethiopians with a pinch of salt; Middle Eastern countries usually add cardamom and spices; and whipped cream is the favorite among Austrians. No matter the method, coffee culture makes for a unique, interesting and, most importantly, tasty story rooted in history and steeped in culture.

AUSTRIA

Doing Nothing Is Taken Seriously

Ordering from a coffee house waiter is considered a cultural rite in Austria. In Vienna, it is still common today for some *conditoras*, or coffee house waiters, to adhere to the traditional 18th-century tradition of coming to the table with a color chart. With a dizzying array of 20 different varieties of brown from which to choose, a surefire way to give yourself away as a tourist is to order a plain, regular cup of coffee. Café-goers can try coffee with liqueurs, ice cream or *kaisermelange*, which is mocha with an egg yolk, honey and cognac or brandy instead of milk.

No matter the type of coffee ordered, it is always accompanied by a glass of ice-cold water. This is a custom that started during the days of the Turkish occupation, but now reflects the belief that nothing goes better with Viennese coffee and cakes than their crisp, fresh water. It is completely normal—nay, expected—for a guest to linger in a coffee house for hours on end, reading the newspaper, writing a book or relaxing, only ever having purchased a single cup of coffee. The friendly Viennese waiters apparently encourage one's long and leisurely stay by bringing a fresh glass of cold water every half-hour as a kind of time-clock courtesy.

This *Kaffeehauskultur* (coffee house culture) is taken very seriously and, reportedly, Viennese waiters are required to have a certain tableside manner known as *schmäh*, or Viennese humor. It's not enough just to be able to order coffee, it is much more important to enjoy yourself while doing it! Whether the reality of present-day coffee houses supports this coffee utopia remains to be seen. It may be another one of coffee's great legends, but the research might be fun.

Here's a sample menu from the Restaurant Kronprinz Rudolph:

- **Brauner:** black coffee with milk
- **Espresso:** black coffee from the espresso-machine
- **Einspänner:** double espresso with whipped cream
- **Mokka or Schwarzer:** black coffee without milk or cream
- **Kurzer or Shorty:** mocha prepared with less water
- **Verläengerter:** mocha prepared with more water
- **Mokka Gespritzt:** mocha with a little rum or brandy
- **Pharisäer:** large mocha with a little rum and whipped cream
- **Melange:** large coffee with hot milk foam
- **Mit Schlagobers:** hot chocolate served with sugar-and-vanilla-flavored whipped cream
- **Kapuziner:** small mocha with some drops of cream
- **Kaffee Verkehrt:** small mocha infused with hot milk and milk foam
- **Mazagran:** coffee with maraschino cherries, spices and liquid sugar, served cold with ice-cubes in a special glass
- **Schale Gold:** coffee mixed with cream until golden-brown
- **Fiaker:** double espresso with powdered sugar, cherry brandy, heavy cream and a maraschino cherry

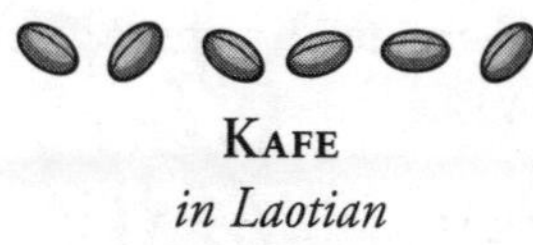

Kafe
in Laotian

FRANCE

Parisians like coffee more than they do sex, cinema or Charles de Gaulle.

–Sanche de Gramont, historian

Sweet Teeth

Though the French are well known for being avid coffee drinkers, they are also equally famous for drinking terrible coffee. Surprised? The stereotypical vision of Paris may involve romantic encounters in cafés by the Seine, but in reality, the French like their coffee strong, thick and unbearably sweet.

And while it's true that the café is alive with conversation and lingering patrons savoring tiny cups of espresso, the most popular way of drinking coffee is at home in cups the size of cereal bowls. Homemade percolated coffee is served with enough sugar to make Willy Wonka jealous. The French adore coffee almost as much as they do wine, and the beverage is so acceptable that even two-year-old children are given a cup of coffee every morning at breakfast.

In rural villages throughout France, coffee is served in all the bars. They are more family friendly and community-oriented than in North America and are often the heart of small-town French life. Villagers come in for their newspapers, bread and daily gossip.

Ordering a coffee in France will get you a small cup of very strong black coffee. And heads up visitors, ordering a *café au lait* in France will likely get you a blank stare from your waiter. Although the French have started bowing to the requests of tourists, it has never been customary to mix coffee with milk in France.

You will have to learn how to ask for a *café crème*, which is a large cup of coffee with hot cream. You can also request a *ralongé* which means they will "make it longer" by adding hot water. If you do ask for milk, it is always served in a separate pot and is usually cold unless you ask for it to be heated first.

Some of France's specialties include the following:

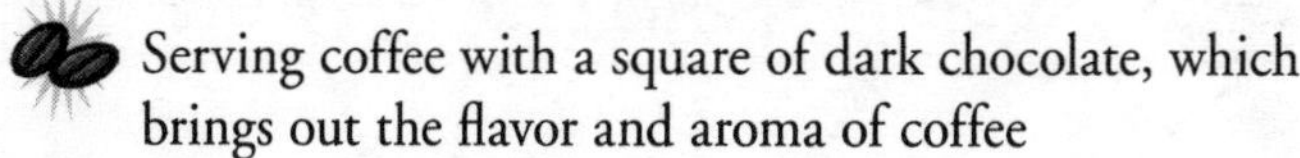
Serving coffee with a square of dark chocolate, which brings out the flavor and aroma of coffee

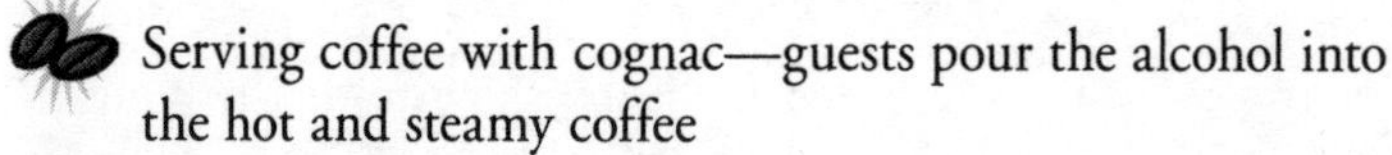
Serving coffee with cognac—guests pour the alcohol into the hot and steamy coffee

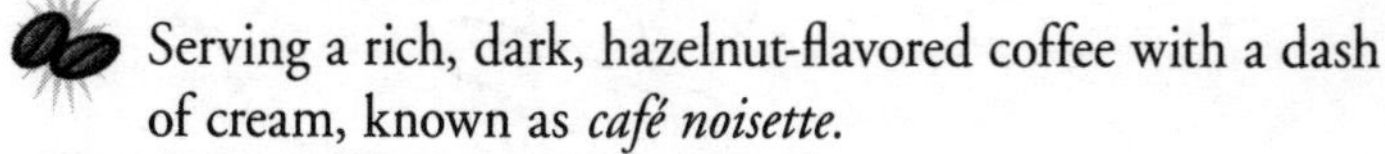
Serving a rich, dark, hazelnut-flavored coffee with a dash of cream, known as *café noisette.*

FINLAND

Winter Warmer

Finns drink coffee anywhere and everywhere: at home, at work, visiting friends, entertaining friends, doing the shopping, at the gas station, mowing the grass, hunting, shooting and fishing—any excuse will do to get their hands on that coffee cup. And, with a winter that lasts anywhere from three to seven months, it's no surprise! The Finns themselves claim that coffee is an essential component of not only learning how to survive the winter in Finland, but enjoying it as well.

Dedicated Drinkers

People in Finland drink more coffee per person than anywhere else in the world. In 2004, the average Finn drank about four cups of coffee a day, or 26.5 pounds per year. Compare that to 17.8 pounds per person in Sweden, 9.5 pounds per person in the U.S., 7.5 pounds in Japan and 5 pounds in Great Britain.

DID YOU KNOW?

Light-roasted coffee is actually more potent than dark roast. Dark roast simply means that the bean has been roasted to a higher temperature for a longer period of time. Finnish coffee is light-roasted, and therefore more bitter, and is slightly stronger than coffee drunk in Europe or America.

Finnish Finesse

Serving coffee is a very important Finnish custom. The Finns have a coffee ceremony in which they drink their coffee through sugar cubes held in the mouth. The table is elaborately decorated with beautiful coffee cups and an array of pastries, cakes, biscuits or other goodies. As in North America, most family celebrations, special occasions, receptions or visits by friends involve coffee.

Drinking coffee in the parish hall after church services is so important that it is jokingly referred to as the third sacrament of the Finnish Lutheran Church.

The café culture may not be as prominent as in Vienna or Paris, but Helsinki does have some excellent coffee houses. Café Succès, for example, is known not only for its outstanding coffee but also for serving *korvapuusti*, the world's largest cinnamon buns.

So grab your parka and your snowmobile—it might be worth a visit.

Kawa
in Polish

ETHIOPIA

Buna dabo naw (Coffee is our bread)

–Ethiopian proverb

Nothing Instant Served Here

If Finland is too cold and snowy, you may want to pack your bags and head to the birthplace of coffee, Ethiopia, which is still steeped in a rich coffee tradition. Ethiopia stands out as one of the few African countries that consumes a large proportion of its own high-quality coffee. Here, the coffee is often roasted, ground and brewed by hand. Just as the Japanese have an elaborate tea ceremony, so do the Ethiopians with coffee.

Ethiopia's coffee ceremony is an integral part of the social and cultural life. An invitation to attend a coffee ceremony is considered a gesture of friendship, respect and goodwill. The hospitality of the Ethiopians, though, may be lost on the visitor in a hurry—this special ceremony can take a couple of hours, so sit back, enjoy and savor the flavor.

Just as in North America and most of Europe, it is unimaginable for most Ethiopians to start a new day without several cups of coffee. As a general rule, most Ethiopian farmers will not start the morning's work on their farms without first drinking a cup of coffee, even if they've had nothing to eat.

But if you think that the ceremony is reserved especially for guests, you'd be mistaken. The Ethiopians revere their coffee so highly that they often indulge in daily coffee ceremonies all by themselves, or just with the neighbors. It is traditionally believed that the Ethiopian coffee ceremony takes place as a ritual to honor the good spirit of the house.

Sacred Sipping Ceremony

The *jebena*, a clay kettle, and the *mukecha*, a wooden coffee-grinding tool, are traditional and handmade. Electric coffee grinders and aluminum kettles are never used, even if women have the means to buy them, because it is believed that modern machines might spoil the natural taste of the bean. No matter their socio-economic status, all Ethiopian women have coffee utensils at the ready for daily use.

Traditionally, beans were roasted on a flat clay utensil known as a *mitad*, but nowadays, a small, flat, circular dish is used for roasting coffee, which is washed several times by hand before it is roasted. The beans are then pounded to a powder using the *mukecha*.

Once the coffee has been prepared, it is brought to a corner of the house specially reserved for coffee ceremonies. The corner is cleaned and sprinkled with freshly cut grass before the utensils are brought in; the fresh grass is a symbol of good luck.

Blessed Beverage

According to Dean Cycon in his book *Javatrekker*, before each coffee ceremony an ancient Ethiopian blessing called the *beraka* is said, in which the drinkers give thanks to the many hands that have touched all that is set before them, contributing to its nurture, fruition and delivery.

The coffee is usually served on a wooden or aluminum tray along with a dozen or more small white ceramic cups. Incense burning is also an integral part of the ceremony. As soon as the kettle with the boiling coffee leaves the fire, the incense is lit and placed near the door on a small piece of clay. The smoke wafts out the door, and the host whispers a few words of thanks to the good spirit of the house, known as the *ad bar*. Prayers are said, wishing the day to be a peaceful and enjoyable one, for the sick to get well and the poor to find jobs.

A snack of roasted grain, bread or a piece of *injera*—a round pancake made of a special Ethiopian grain grass known as *teff*—is brought to the guests before the coffee is served. The host then pours a few drops into each cup to be emptied onto the floor as an offering to the *ad bar*, which is believed to be present in the house every time coffee is served.

What makes the Ethiopian coffee ceremony quite unique and interesting is that coffee is served three times in a row. Called *abol*, *tona* and *baraka*, the water is reboiled and served three times to the guests, the only difference being that the coffee becomes thinner and weaker after each round of boiling. Guests are expected to stay seated until the coffee ceremony is over, and it is impolite to walk out in the middle of a ceremony.

At the end of the ceremony, everyone present joins in a blessing, wishing all the guests good health, wealth and a peaceful time. All the utensils used during the coffee ceremony are then washed and properly arranged in anticipation of the next ceremony.

Unlike the Japanese tea ceremony, which can be prepared by a woman or a man, it is taboo in Ethiopia for men to boil coffee.

ITALY

The Art of Coffee

No one knows coffee like the Italians. They lavish an enormous amount of energy on just about everything they do, from love-making to pasta to the art of a perfect cup of coffee. It should come as no surprise that the most popular form of coffee in Italy is by far the espresso, though the word is never used since ordering a *caffè* will always get you an espresso.

From big city to mountain village, it is widely accepted and well known that the Italians are the unrivalled world masters of espresso. Very few people know, however, about the little brother of the espresso, the *espressino.* The espressino is served cold and is found primarily in southern Italy, perfect for its hot summers and probably really fun to order.

At the Caffè degli Specchi in Trieste, a 19th-century grand caffè on the city's main piazza, customers are offered 67 different kinds of coffee, each with a specific name.

When in Rome

Follow the lead of locals and stand at the bar, thus avoiding the service charge. Romans don't linger over their espressos. They tend to dive-bomb into their local coffee houses, drink their espresso like a shooter and get back to the business of the day. Locals recommend curbing your cappuccino cravings before 10:00 AM—ordering the drink any later is sacrilege for Italians, who consider cappuccino solely a breakfast beverage.

The Italian term *barista*, meaning bartender, is now used worldwide to designate someone talented in the art of making a good cup of coffee, but in Italy and elsewhere in Europe, a *barista* is still someone who is skilled in making *all* kinds of beverages, not just coffee-flavored ones.

BOSNIA AND HERZEGOVINA

Like an Espresso but Stronger

The Ottoman rule of the former Yugoslavia in the 14th century left many traces of Turkish traditions all across the region, including a love of coffee. Today, coffee in Bosnia is described as the backbone of social life by travel writer Tim Clancy: "Believe it or not, this country may be the only place on Earth where the largest profit margin from any product sold in a country comes from coffee sales—and they don't even grow it here." Coffee drinking is considered an everyday social event and is not just an individual habit, as may be the case in North America.

Nowadays, coffee is widely available and affordable. Small coffee houses are known as *kafano*, in which the owners take your order, brew and serve your coffee while you wait. The traditional coffee is called *bosanska kafa*, and it is prepared like Turkish coffee—the grounds are boiled and allowed to settle, and the drink is served strong and thick.

When it is done correctly, *bosanska kafa* can be a unique coffee experience, though confused visitors often make a mess of the ritual since most of them have never been shown how to drink it properly. The coffee is usually served in a long-handled open metal pot known as a *džezva* (pronounced "jezva") coupled with a small round cup called a *fildžan* (pronounced "filljohn"), along with sugar cubes and a candy on a copper plate. The coffee is poured into tiny demitasse-type cups.

Don't Swallow the Last Sip!

Before drinking, you first need to stir the top layer of coffee in the *džezva*. Once it turns a rich cream color, it is ready to be poured. The *džezva* is usually filled with a little more coffee than the *fildžan* can hold because you want to leave a small amount of coffee at the bottom to avoid getting a mouthful of grounds, which are lurking at the bottom. The glass of water you get with the coffee isn't really meant for washing down the gritty bits, but it'll do the trick if you forget. Traditionally, the sugar cubes are dipped into the cup and eaten, though it is acceptable to dissolve them in the coffee before drinking it.

Most places serve the coffee with a piece of jelly-like candy called *rahat lokum*. Similar to Turkish delight, it is coated with powdered sugar; however, the candy is not meant to be dipped into the coffee, nor is the copper plate meant to be used as a saucer.

So, although Bosnia may not be known the world over for the caliber of its coffee, the way they prepare it and the reverence with which the coffee is treated has led some residents to claim that the Bosnians have "the best coffee in the world."

Just as in Britain, where "having tea" means a small dinner, one cannot enter a Bosnian house without being offered coffee, which also includes a small meal. It is also not uncommon for Bosnians to serve their coffee with a little watermelon on the side.

Minas Coffee: From Bosnia, With Love

Some coffee connoisseurs might be interested in getting their hands on a cup of Minas coffee from Bosnia. It has been said that Minas is to coffee as tomatoes are to fruit—just as you may not know that tomatoes are fruit, you might not recognize Minas as being coffee. Reportedly, the flavor is unlike any other coffee you've ever had before.

The Balkan coffee is prepared Turkish-style and is very finely ground, producing the smoothest cup of coffee you'll ever taste. It doesn't have a high amount of caffeine in it and, even more appealing for coffee snobs, it's quite difficult to get your hands on.

Oddly enough, Minas is also the name of a large coffee-producing state in Brazil. Speculation is that the Bosnian coffee is called Minas because Yugoslavians bought up extensive estates in that region of Brazil many years ago. The price is relatively gentle on the pocketbook, only $11.99 for a two-pound bag.

DID YOU KNOW?

In Bosnia, some manual coffee grinders are made from used grenade shells leftover from the war in Sarajevo. Even though some of these shells might not *really* be from Sarajevo, it is generally regarded as a positive use of these former weapons of war.

KAFEI
in Mandarin

TURKEY

Grounds for Divorce

For centuries, coffee has dominated social life in Turkey, influencing everything from gender roles to marriage rituals, from prayer and hospitality to political and social interactions. In the past, harem women were meticulously trained in the proper method of preparing Turkish coffee. The merits of a future wife, in fact, were oftentimes based solely on the quality of her coffee. During the courting period, prospective husbands, male relatives and friends would come over to literally "taste her goods."

Once they were married, though, the tides quickly turned, and it was now the Turkish bridegroom who was required to present coffee to his new wife. In fact, should a Turkish husband fail to provide his wife with coffee, Turkish law permitted the woman to divorce him for failing to keep the family *cezve*—a traditional brass pot—filled. Luckily for the men, this is no longer a law, though they still take pride in doing it—making coffee, that is. Nowadays, however, tea is increasingly more prevalent than coffee along the shores of this Middle Eastern country.

THE MIDDLE EAST

The Coffee Ritual

Nowhere in the world is coffee is more indispensable to life than in the Middle East. Just a little over a century ago, American author Mark Twain made a trip to Jerusalem. While there, he observed that "the people drink coffee on awakening and then continue drinking coffee through the entire day. No business deal can be closed, no one can become a friend, and no one can be seduced without the presence of coffee. With the Good Lord as my witness, they even serve coffee at their funerals."

Not much has changed in the past 100 years.

The coffee ritual in Arabian countries begins with green coffee beans called *bunnu*, which are roasted and then finely ground with a mortar and pestle. The ground coffee is then boiled in a coffeepot called a *dallah* with cardamom seeds, sugar and sometimes a pinch of saffron or cloves—milk is never added. Cardamom comes in little seedpods, which are ground up and brewed with the coffee. Another method is to strain the liquid and pour it through cardamom pods as you are serving it.

Spicing Things Up

Cardamom was, and still is, an expensive spice and actually costs more than coffee itself—the wealthier you were, the more cardamom you used. This meant that sometimes coffee contained as much as 90 percent cardamom, leaving the remaining percentage of coffee to drown unnoticed in a yellow, super-sweet brew. As such, Arabian countries have at times consumed as much as 80 percent of the world's total cardamom exports.

Although cardamom is native to India and Sri Lanka, the largest commercial producer today is Guatemala, which started growing the spice in the 1920s. In some areas of the country, cardamom has replaced coffee as the most important crop.

In much of the Arab world, the common way to make coffee is to take a spoonful of the ground coffee, mix it with water in a *kanakah*—a fluted, long-handled, copper pot—and bring it to a boil over the stove. The coffee is poured into small cups called *finjaan*.

Either way, you produce what the Arabs call Arabic coffee and what the rest of the world refers to as Turkish coffee.

Coffee Houses

Since Turkish coffee was first introduced into the Ottoman Empire during the 15th century, the sultans forbade the drinking of coffee because, according to the strictest rule of the Qur'an, it was considered a drug. However, in spite of the restriction, drinking coffee became so popular that the palace rescinded the rule and allowed its consumption.

Coffee houses are still very popular in the Arab world, being a place to sit and speak with friends, drink tea or coffee and play backgammon or dominoes. Today, like Turks, Arabs actually drink more tea than coffee. In the past, storytellers would come and tell stories in the coffee houses, but now most storytellers have been replaced by television or radio. To this day, there are still devout followers of the Islamic faith will not visit a coffee house, as per the Qur'an.

EGYPT

The Sheesha

Egyptians are extremely fond of pure, strong coffee. The way in which coffee is served even varies depending on the event. For example, unsweetened coffee is served to mourners at a funeral, while sweetened coffee is poured at weddings.

Today, tourists often seek out Egyptian coffee houses for a special cultural experience—the *sheesha*. Using a hookah, a water-based smoking pipe that is packed with the sheesha, a special blend of fresh, dark tobacco leaves, fruit pulp, honey or molasses and glycerin, tourists can smoke their way through a wide variety of flavors, including cappuccino, mint, apricot, apple, strawberry, melon, pineapple, vanilla, pistachio, rose—the list goes on and on. Contrary to popular opinion, the blend contains no tar and very little nicotine—only 0.5 percent—and no, you won't get high.

According to the custom, smoking the sheesha is more so about taking time to socialize with friends, to slow down and enjoy the company. Although in larger centers such as Cairo it is perfectly acceptable for women to enter the coffee house and smoke the sheesha, it is traditionally an activity reserved exclusively for the men.

If the sheesha is too reminiscent of your college days for your liking, you'll do just fine sticking to coffee, also known as *qahwe turki*. Turkish coffee can be ordered plain (*sâda*), sweet (*helwa*), medium sweet (*masbout*) or with a bit of sugar (*sukr khafeef*). However, be forewarned—sweet coffee in this country is not an exaggeration!

It is estimated that more than 20,000 coffee houses can be found in Cairo. As of today, the downtown and Islamic sections of Cairo are some of the best locations to enjoy this important and special piece of Egyptian culture.

SPAIN AND PORTUGAL

Cake in a Cup

Rim a tall heavy glass mug with sugar, then drizzle in a little Galliano. Add brandy and some Cointreau. Next, top it with whipped cream. Sound like a delicious dessert? Well, before Starbucks came along with their brand of hot coffee milkshakes, there was Spanish coffee. It was the old-school way for our parents to take coffee and kick it up a notch.

And for those of you who enjoy a little Baileys in your coffee on Christmas morning, we likely also have the Spanish to thank. Whether the Spaniards were the originators of adding alcohol to coffee is not known conclusively, but the practice is still very common there, even today.

Coffee originally came to Spain with Turkish immigrants. Very little coffee was ever really grown in Spain, but they developed a method for roasting beans that produced very dark, almost black, oily beans that made for a very strong cup of coffee, now known as Spanish Roast.

Early Arabic coffee traders tended to gouge the Spanish coffee merchants, which meant that Spain boasted the most expensive cup of coffee in Europe. Portugal, Spain's neighbor, had colonies in several coffee-growing regions of Africa and sold coffee to Spain at more reasonable prices; however, the quality was not quite as good, and some importers willingly chose to pay the higher prices for Arabian coffee.

Spanish ships brought coffee plants and seeds to many remote areas of the world, and the descendants of Spanish conquistadors settled in Central and South America, where huge plantations for growing Spanish coffee were created. Most years, Spanish coffee growers in Latin America account for nearly half of all the coffee exported.

A Coffee Way of Life

Today, coffee is part of every meal in Spain and Portugal. Most coffee served in Spain comes from Angola and Mozambique and is still roasted super-dark to bring out its full flavor. Most families have a small espresso machine in their homes, and nearly every adult wakes up to a small cup of very strong, syrupy-sweet coffee in the morning. At breakfast, coffee is served again, usually in large cups with steaming milk and sometimes just a hint of brandy. In the afternoon and early evening, coffee is drunk black and strong. In the late evening, many take yet another cup of coffee accompanied by a glass of sweet brandy or anisette, a sweet liqueur. Suddenly, that Christmas-morning Baileys and coffee you had doesn't seem so gluttonous!

Coffee houses in Spain most commonly serve espresso. Waiters in white shirts and black ties serve delicious coffee in elaborate and elegant surroundings. Customers are dressed respectfully, and the atmosphere is somewhat more reserved than in coffee houses in other regions of the world, where the environment is more casual and informal.

In Southern Spain and Gibraltar, locals swear that their coffee is bar none and just can't be duplicated outside the Costa del Sol.

CAFEA
in Latin

IRELAND

Only Irish coffee provides in a single glass all four essential food groups: alcohol, caffeine, sugar and fat.
–Alex Levine, Irish actor and musician

Irish Coffee: A Modern Invention

Coffee, whiskey, sugar and thick cream—the original Irish coffee was invented by Joseph Sheridan on a cold and blustery winter night in the 1940s. Air travel was still relatively new and, in the days before the construction of Shannon International Airport, a trip to Ireland might've included taking a seaplane to the port of Foynes, followed by a chilly boat ride from the plane to the terminal.

Sheridan was the head chef at the airport in Foynes, a port town in southwestern Ireland. The story goes that one night Sheridan decided to help some exhausted, bedraggled American passengers keep warm by adding a bit of whiskey to their coffee. After being asked if they were being served Brazilian coffee, Sheridan replied, "No, it's Irish coffee."

Every summer, the people of Foynes celebrate the Irish Coffee Festival, which is a free street festival featuring Irish entertainers, parades, a carnival, traditional Irish music and fireworks over the River Shannon. The highlight of the festival is the World Irish Coffee Championship, with contestants from Ireland and around the world competing to win the honor of best Irish coffee.

Coming to America

Stanton Delaplane, a travel writer for *The San Francisco Chronicle*, claims to have brought Irish coffee to the United States in 1952 when he started the laborious chore of recreating an authentic Irish coffee for the Buena Vista Café. However, Tom Bergin's

Tavern in Los Angeles claims to have been serving Irish coffee a full two years before the Buena Vista.

Whoever started making it first, it was the Buena Vista Café that perfected the American Irish coffee, painstakingly achieved after many taste tests, a return trip to Ireland and a personal consultation with the mayor of San Francisco, who also happened to be a dairy owner. The problem with Delaplane's Irish coffee was that the cream kept sinking to the bottom, but they eventually discovered that, when the cream was aged for 48 hours and frothed properly, it floated perfectly on top. The Buena Vista Café is now world famous for its Irish coffees and sells more per day than anywhere else in the world.

But really, does anyone truly care where Irish coffee came from? After a couple of them, no one will even remember, anyway. Bottoms up!

JAPAN

Coveting Coffee

Though it is typically known as a tea-loving nation, Japan has actually had a long tradition of coffee houses called *kissaten*, with Tokyo alone home to over 10,000. This dates back to the end of the 19th century when, during the Meiji era, a new cultural awakening was felt in Japan and one of the more unlikely items at its forefront was coffee. Since then, Japan has become a mind-boggling consumer of coffee and today it's the world's third largest importer. In 2008, Japan purchased a staggering 387,538 tons of green coffee beans and 6652 tons of roasted coffee beans, a 14 percent increase from 2007.

Why? Well, the Japanese are well known for coveting the best of just about everything the world has to offer, and coffee is no exception. Their penchant for rare and exotic things means that much of the most sought-after coffee on earth ends up in the Japanese market. For example, Japan buys more than 90 percent of Jamaican Blue Mountain for its eager and thirsty citizens. This has made Japan the seventh largest coffee retail market in the world, snapping at the heels of the more traditional coffee lovers, including the Italians.

Coffee is not only more popular in both volume and value terms, but even overall tea sales are losing ground to coffee, exhibiting a consistent decline over the last 20 years.

Fresh Cup, Canned Cup, Instant Cup

In what may be a uniquely Japanese consumer quirk, different kinds of coffee—such as canned, regular and instant—are considered to be completely different types of beverages. In the U.S., all types of coffee are generally lumped together, but in Japan, coffee drinkers are likely to choose different types of coffee depending on their desire.

Most of the time, once Americans make the leap from instant coffee to roasted or fresh-ground coffee, there is no turning back. But the Japanese are likely to drink all different types of coffee at different times.

October 1 is official Coffee Day in Japan. Coffee Day is a veritable fiesta, featuring coffee samples in the streets and performances in major cities throughout Japan. National Coffee Day varies from country to country. In Costa Rica, it is on September 12, while Ireland raises a cup to the holy bean on September 19.

Canned Coffee

The Japanese invented canned coffee, which is dispensed by vending machines in both hot and cold versions. Of Japan's total coffee imports, one-third is used in the production of canned coffee and half of the remaining volume is used to manufacture instant coffee. In fact, everywhere you turn in Japan, you will be able to find brightly glowing vending machines filled with warm cans of coffee, tea or the obvious alternative—corn chowder. Sure, the hot aluminum tin may be a little hard to hold at first, but it's all part of the cultural experience.

Starbucks in Japan

High-quality coffee is also very popular in Japan. Here, Starbucks is lovingly referred to as "Sta-ba," with an endearing and phonetically correct "bente" to order a venti coffee, which is about one-third the size of its North American equivalent. Starbucks is as popular for its coffee as it is for the spacious seating arrangements and non-smoking environment. A cup of coffee in Japan is quite expensive, even by Starbucks standards, but the Japanese aren't just paying for the coffee—theye paying for the space to sit down for a while and savor the flavor. The non-smoking environment has also proven to be a big selling point in a nation that currently has very few restrictions on smoking in public restaurants and bars.

"Sta-ba" may have given coffee drinking in Japan a new lease on life, but it did not introduce good coffee to Japan. It was the sophisticated café-lounge concept that caught on with the locals and, as Japan was already one of the world's highest consumers of coffee, it's easy to see why international coffee companies chose Japan as a "strategic" coffee-selling market.

If It Ain't Broke, Make It Better Anyway

The Japanese, to their credit, don't take an idea and merely transplant it. The rapid spread of Starbucks and other new-style coffee bars has prompted many to pass the trend off as another example of globalization. But upon closer inspection, the Japanese have once again demonstrated the artful craftsmanship their culture has come to master—the ability to soak up new ideas and inventions, give them an extensive makeover and then add a uniquely Japanese twist.

Most people are familiar with the old adage: "If it ain't broke, don't fix it." This, you see, does not align with the Japanese way of thinking at all. Throughout the entire history of their culture, the Japanese have refined the art of fixing unbroken things to perfection and beyond. In the case of the café boom, the Japanese have elevated coffee to their own exacting high standards.

Manga Houses

Some Japanese coffee houses have unique themes to distinguish themselves from their competition. Music coffee shops, for example, featuring jazz, classical or rock music, have always been favorite hangouts for the younger crowd since their inception in the early 1960s.

Less mainstream are the manga (comic book) coffee houses that have sprung up in recent years in Tokyo. Coffee is served for free, and customers are only required to pay a small entrance fee for the time spent reading the manga comics lining the walls—it is even permitted to bring your own meal!

Don't Kissa and Tell

On a similar theme, "Maid Kissa" coffee shops feature beautiful young waitresses wearing maid costumes that resemble characters from famous anime and manga. Customers are welcomed in by

the somewhat strange greeting "Welcome home, my master." In addition to the verbal role-play, maids pour coffee and tea for patrons and play cards if requested. Many of these coffee shops are decorated in the style of an English mansion to make customers truly feel like the "master of the house." Certainly, by Western standards, this type of role-playing would seem awkward, and the name of the establishment makes its purpose sound dubious, but actually "kissa" is merely short for *kissaten*, the name for a Japanese coffee shop.

DID YOU KNOW?

Tiger Woods was once a spokesperson for Wonda Coffee, a Tokyo-based company—and it turns out that he's not alone. There's been no shortage of foreign celebrities happy to be flown in first-class to lend their name to a range of products in exchange for a handsome fee and, more importantly, the assurance that their endorsements would not be seen outside Japan (unfortunately for the celebs, this deal was struck before the advent of YouTube). Kiefer Sutherland has advertised the health snack CalorieMate, Brad Pitt has donned a pair of Levi's 501 jeans and Richard Gere has endorsed a men's beauty spa called Dandy House. There is even a term for this type of celebrity endorsement—it is called a "Japander." A Japander is a western star that uses his or her fame to make large sums of money in a short time by advertising products in Japan that they would probably never be caught dead endorsing anywhere else in the world.

Cafe
in Portuguese

CHINA

Uncupped Potential

China is recognized as being the fastest-growing major economy and, while tea and rice wine are still the most popular beverages there, demand for coffee is on the rise—and so is quality. Until recently, the majority of coffee consumed was of the instant variety, but as the number of middle-class consumers rises, so does coffee consumption. Fashionable coffee bars that are popular with young people have begun to surface in Peking, Shanghai and several other major Chinesc cities.

If roasters continue to offer products that suit local consumer budgets and tastes, the market may keep expanding by up to 20 percent a year. In 2008 alone, the number of coffee-roasting companies in China increased from 25 to 30.

In 2008, Starbucks said that China has the potential to become its largest market outside the United States. Indeed, the Chinese market is appealing because potential coffee drinkers in China number somewhere in the 200 million range. This veritable untapped market will leave companies like Starbucks clamoring to be the first to fill their cups to the brim.

Chinese Exports

China produces 25,000 tons of beans a year, of which 5000 tons are the Robusta variety, grown in Hainan and mainly used in instant coffee. The rest are Arabica beans produced in Yunnan and are preferred by coffee house owners for their superior quality.

China sells about 60 percent of its coffee overseas, and half of the exports are sent to Japan for making instant coffee. China also imports about 15,000 tons of coffee a year, including the instant coffee made from their own beans.

NORTH AMERICA

You've Come a Long Way, Baby

In the United States and Canada, the last 15 years or so have seen a coffee revolution. Until then, with the exception of Greenwich Village, Montréal, San Francisco, Seattle and a few other isolated places, the coffee that Americans were drinking was mostly watery, weak and either too bland or fiercely bitter. Europeans tourists visiting the United States pre-1990 would no doubt have found the American version of "coffee" an aberration and not so wrongly convicted it as the devil's brew. Baba Budan was no doubt rolling in his benevolent little grave.

Seattle, also known as Lattetown USA, is generally agreed upon to be the spiritual home of coffee in America. In the 1970s, the city

gave birth to a vibrant café culture that took the country by storm, dramatically improving the general quality of the coffee Americans drink. But why Seattle?

According to author Taylor Clark, there are a few reasons why Seattle is the number one Beantown:

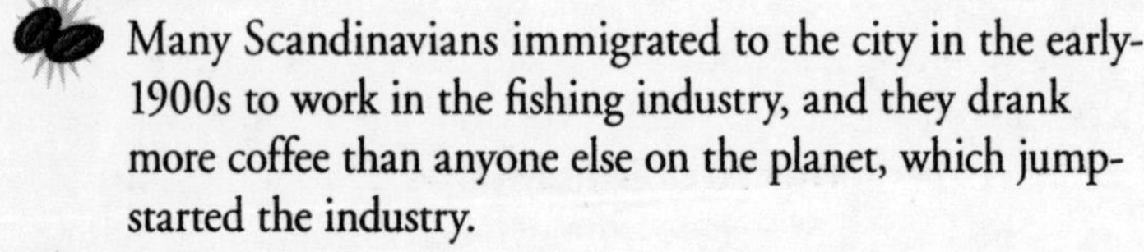

- Many Scandinavians immigrated to the city in the early-1900s to work in the fishing industry, and they drank more coffee than anyone else on the planet, which jump-started the industry.

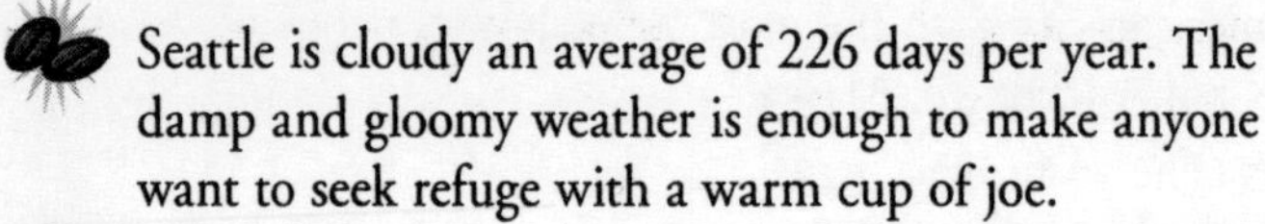

- Seattle is cloudy an average of 226 days per year. The damp and gloomy weather is enough to make anyone want to seek refuge with a warm cup of joe.

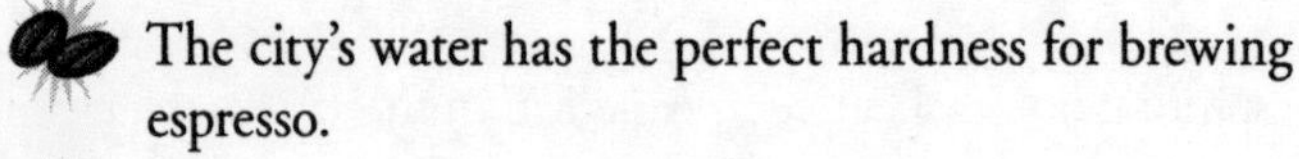

- The city's water has the perfect hardness for brewing espresso.

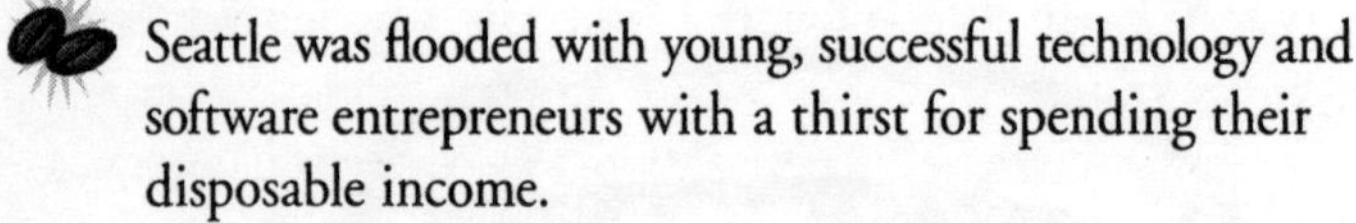

- Seattle was flooded with young, successful technology and software entrepreneurs with a thirst for spending their disposable income.

Quick Facts About Coffee in the United States

- Coffee is not grown anywhere in the continental United States, but the country does boast first-rate growing regions in Hawaii and Puerto Rico.

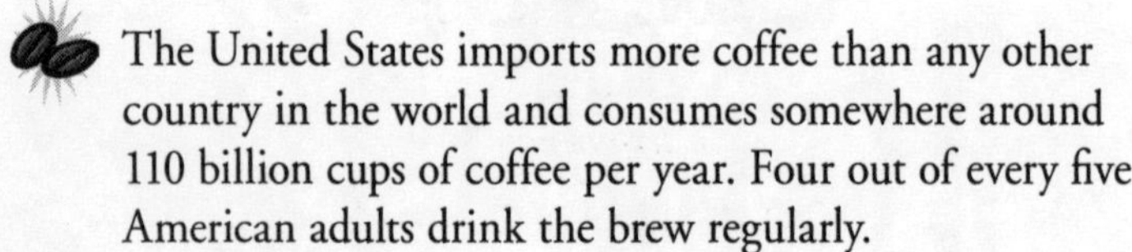

- The United States imports more coffee than any other country in the world and consumes somewhere around 110 billion cups of coffee per year. Four out of every five American adults drink the brew regularly.
- Americans now drink so much coffee that scientists have detected caffeine in many of the nation's rivers, lakes and

bays—sometimes even in treated drinking water!—a residual by-product of human waste.

Even today, the "gourmet coffee revolution" aside, the most popular way of making coffee in America is with the good old-fashioned percolator. Slowly but surely, we're getting there.

The American city with the most coffee houses per capita is not Seattle, but Anchorage, Alaska.

New Orleans Style

During the American Civil War, when coffee was scarce, the citizens of New Orleans began using chicory root as a substitute. Chicory, which can still be found growing in rocky terrain next to highways, can be dried, roasted and ground to make a brew that is strong and bitter. Today, coffee in New Orleans has been popularized by this rich history, and it is common to serve strong, black coffee mixed with chicory and hot, rich milk. The coffee is commonly accompanied by powdered-sugar-covered *beignets*—or doughnuts—the sweetness of which offsets the bitterness of the chicory.

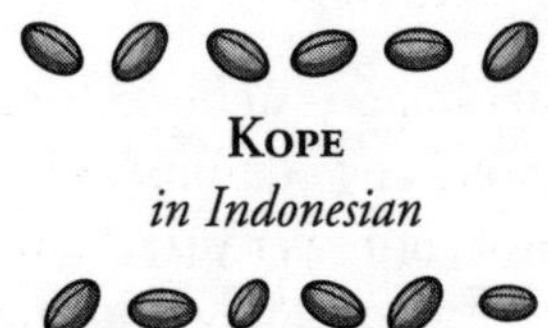

BRAZIL

Unshaded Roasts

Brazil is a coffee giant. The country's coffee industry began in 1727 when Melo Palheta, a military man and diplomat, brought coffee seedlings back from French Guyana and started the country's first coffee plantation. In no time, coffee became Brazil's largest cash crop and today accounts for approximately 40 percent of the world's total coffee supply.

Surprisingly, despite being a world leader, most Brazilian coffee is not considered to be the best in the world—in fact, it is regarded as a common, low-grade Arabica. Why is that? Well, it stems from the fact that, in Brazil, coffee is grown at lower altitudes than Central American coffee, mostly in non-volcanic soils and in non-forested areas that were originally grassland. One reason that Brazil can't provide "shade-grown" coffee is because of the flat farmland on which it is grown, which has little shade to offer.

"Brazils" are not dense coffee beans, meaning that any dark roast picks up an ashy, bitter flavor and, as a result, most Brazilian coffees taste somewhat harsh. Recently, better farming and improved processing techniques have helped the cause, and there has been a big push on behalf of Brazilian coffee-growing associations to re-create an image of Brazilian coffee as a more exquisite and distinctive specialty-grade coffee.

So, does that mean that Brazilian coffee is "bad"? Absolutely not!

Brazil still has fabulous light-roast coffees, and their dry-processed natural coffees produce more crema and body that can add sweetness to espresso blends. Brazils can be nutty, sweet and low acid, and can develop exceptional bittersweet and chocolate roast tastes. The Bourbon Santos coffee beans produce a great cup of coffee, so try pouring yourself a cup.

The Economy Leaves Bitter Taste

Most recently, Brazil's problems have been exacerbated by the economic crunch. Coffee prices rose 24 percent in 2009 because of expectations that production in Brazil and Colombia would drop.

In June 2009, Nestlé S.A.—the biggest buyer of Brazil's coffee and sugar—said that prices may increase even more as growers worldwide fail to invest in expansion and as demand for food increases faster than output.

Nestlé's Brazilian headquarters buys 1.5 million bags of coffee a year, about eight percent of domestic consumption. The government reported on May 7, 2009, that coffee output in Brazil is expected to drop by 15 percent in the current year.

Pouring Into Daily Life

Brazil's coffee sector is a vital part of the country's economy. Today, from Rio de Janeiro and Sao Paolo to the tiniest of jungle villages, coffee is an ever-present facet of life. Brazilians have traditionally made their coffee by boiling it, much as is done in Turkey. In addition to drinking coffee at home, in restaurants and in cafés, thousands of coffee vendors also line the streets of all the large cities, with more than 200 in Rio de Janeiro alone. At any one of these stalls, it is possible to enjoy a quick but well-made cup of coffee for the equivalent of just a few pennies.

Although coffee is produced in more than 14 different regions in the country, it is not the beverage of choice for the majority of Brazilians: rather, that honor is bestowed on *guaraná*, a unique Brazilian soft drink that is produced from dried berries, water and sugar and contains about twice the caffeine found in coffee beans.

In Brazilian Portuguese, breakfast is called *café da manhã*—morning coffee.

MEXICO

Different Tastes

Mexico is a major coffee producer and has a long history of coffee production. Its coffee is grown mainly in the south-central regions of the country. Mexican coffees all taste different depending on the growing conditions—beans from Coatepec and Veracruz taste much different than those from Oaxacan Plumas, which are in turn distinct from the southernmost region of Chiapas. Mexico is one of the largest producers of certified organic coffees and, because of its close proximity, most Mexican coffee is exported to the United States.

Coffee was introduced to Mexico during the 19th century, arriving from Jamaica. Mexican coffee is mainly Arabica, which grows particularly well in the Pacific coastal region of Soconusco, near the Mexico-Guatemala border.

During the 1980s, coffee became Mexico's most valuable export crop. More than two million Mexicans were growing coffee, most barely subsisting—75 percent of Mexican coffee growers worked plots smaller than five acres. These small cultivators still produced about 30 percent of the country's annual harvest, while larger and more efficient farms produced the rest.

Chiapas or Bust

As international coffee prices rose further in 1988, the government encouraged coffee growers, especially in Chiapas, to increase their output and to expand the area under cultivation. To try to bolster coffee production, the government also offered easy credit to coffee growers and converted forested land into *ejidos*—plots of tenured land—for cultivation by poor Mexican coffee growers. In the early 1990s, the southern state of Chiapas was Mexico's most important coffee-growing area, producing 45 percent of the annual crop total of 275,000 tons.

The Altura Coatepec beans grown in Chiapas are highly valued, being the finest grade of Mexican coffee available—"Altura" means "high-grown." Where coffee is concerned, higher always means better, and the high-grown coffees of Mexico are considered among the finest in the Americas.

DID YOU KNOW?

In Mexico and throughout Central America, many prefer to add a small amount of cinnamon to ground coffee before brewing; this adds a distinct flavor and also reduces the acidity.

CENTRAL AMERICA

Costa Rica

Costa Rican coffee has set the standards for fine coffee for the rest of Central and South America. Most coffee in Costa Rica comes from the Caturra coffee variety and is characterized as a bright and full-bodied coffee.

The most famous coffees by region are Tarrazu, Très Rios, Herediá and Alajuela. The Très Rios—or Three Rivers—region near the Pacific coast produces coffees that are mild, sweet and bright. The Tarrazu region, which is located in the interior mountains of Costa Rica, produces a relatively heavy coffee with more aromatic complexity.

There's Gold in Them There Hills!

La Minita Estate coffee is the most sought-after coffee in all of Costa Rica. *La Minita* is Spanish for "little mine," and the property is undoubtedly a gold mine, producing some of the best coffee in the world. And even better for penny-pinching java guzzlers: according to specialty coffee roastmaster Jim Cameron, who extols the virtues of the "original" organic fair-trade coffee, the best coffees are not always the most expensive, and La Minita is one of them.

La Minita comes from the Tarrazu region of Costa Rica in Central America. This region has long been known for its quality coffee and remains one of the finest growing regions in the world. The La Minita Estate actually has several microclimates within the farm, which affects the crop in different ways.

The meticulous way in which the coffee is grown, pruned, fertilized, shaded and weeded all add to the quality of the final product. Long before "organic" was popular, this farm was using machetes rather than chemicals to control weeds. Long before "fair trade" was the thing to do, this farm was treating its employees with respect, providing dental and medical resources right on the farm, paying above local scale, providing household items at below-cost prices and encouraging a coffee workers' association to promote fair, safe and equitable working conditions.

Every La Minita coffee bean arrives at the mill the same day it is picked, which is essential in producing the world's best coffee. The milling process is more meticulous than at other mills, and the beans are watched at each stage of the preparation. When they have reached the point where most beans would be bagged and exported, those at La Minita enter their final stage. Every bean is examined by trained coffee sorters, who go over the beans and remove each and every one that may taint the final cup (stinkers, foxes, sours and blacks).

So unlike some other "exotic" coffees of the world such as Kona and Jamaica Blue Mountain, which cost you more because of their reputation rather than the goodness of their bean, La Minita is in this category for one reason and one reason only—its *quality*!

Panama

Looking to splurge? Maybe thinking about trying a coffee that everyone should have at least once in their lifetime? Then try La Esmerelda Especial. This coffee was described as "God in a cup" by Don Holly, quality control manager for Green Mountain Coffee in Vermont.

In 2004, Hacienda La Esmerelda rose to fame after one of its coffees—a rare heirloom varietal of Arabica called "geisha"—won the Best of Panama coffee competition, causing buyers to swoon and prices to soar. With chocolate and berries and a bright flavor, Esmeralda has a profile that doesn't match the mild one typical of Central American coffees. Indeed, the geisha plant is believed to have originated in Ethiopia and to have been introduced to Costa Rica and Panama, where it grows today. To brew yourself a cup of God at home, however, it will cost you around $85 for eight ounces of beans.

Guatemala

Guatemala is one of the most climatically diverse regions in the world. The soil, rainfall, humidity, altitude and temperature are varied enough to produce seven distinct types of Guatemala Arabica coffee, according to the experts at www.coffeeresearch.org.

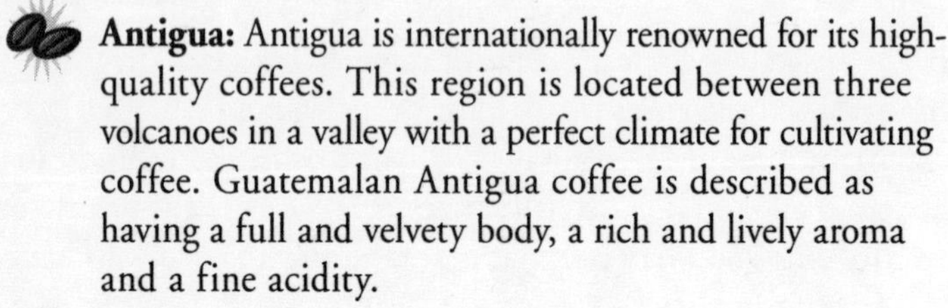

Antigua: Antigua is internationally renowned for its high-quality coffees. This region is located between three volcanoes in a valley with a perfect climate for cultivating coffee. Guatemalan Antigua coffee is described as having a full and velvety body, a rich and lively aroma and a fine acidity.

Fraijanes Plateau: Recent volcanic activity from Volcan de Pacaya deposited ashes rich in minerals into this area, leaving a soil that is rich in potassium, which lends more body to the cup. The combination of altitude, temperature and humidity produces a Strictly Hard coffee bean (the highest rating in Guatemala) and is very similar to a genuine Guatemala Antigua coffee.

Rainforest Cobán: This zone in the northern part of the country is defined as very humid, subtropical forest. In fact, the name Cobán comes from the Maya Keckchi word *cob*, which means "the place of clouds."

Highland Huehuetenango: This region is located on the border with Mexico. Dry, hot winds from the Tehuantepec plain in Mexico protect the region from frost and create its unique microclimate. The humid subtropical climate contributes to the coffee beans' beautiful appearance and uniform maturation.

Atitlan: This area encompasses all the land surrounding Lake Atitlan. Coffee is mainly harvested on the Pacific side in a region with three volcanic mountains and high precipitation. There is no month during which Atitlan will have less than 50 millimeters of rain, and humidity always hovers around 70 to 80 percent. Most producers in this region use water from the lake for wet processing and, instead of chemicals, organic matter is often used as a fertilizer. The high altitude means fewer pests and diseases. Drying takes place almost totally in the sun, and 95 percent of the coffee is cultivated by small producers who have an average plot of 30 acres.

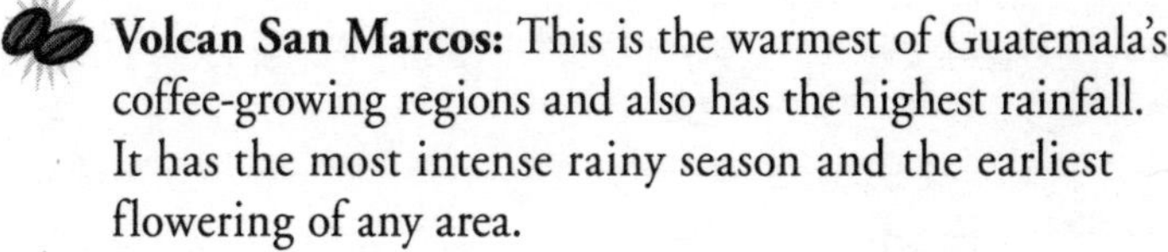

- **Volcan San Marcos:** This is the warmest of Guatemala's coffee-growing regions and also has the highest rainfall. It has the most intense rainy season and the earliest flowering of any area.
- **Oriente:** The weather here is similar to Cobán, but is less intense. It is located over a volcanic range, and the soil consists mainly of metamorphic rock and clay. This area has relatively little rainfall compared to Cobán or San Marcos.

Honduras and Nicaragua

Coffee from Honduras is wet-processed, typically unremarkable in quality and is a good base for blending. Since few Honduran coffee beans ever reach America, you will probably not have the opportunity to compare this coffee with other Central American coffees.

In Nicaragua, coffee was introduced in the mid-19th century. Unfortunately, Nicaraguan coffee has lost some of the valuable characteristics that once made it a sought-after bestseller. The wet-processed Nicaraguan coffee bean has become milder, but still has a light acidity and can be used for blending and dark roasting.

In Honduras, Guatemala and farther south in Panama, a small amount of cocoa is often added to coffee.

Central American Coffee Crisis

In 2001, a steep drop in coffee prices on the world market led to a crisis in Central America during which coffee growers either scaled back or closed down, leaving approximately 300,000 Nicaraguan coffee-field workers in the lurch.

The crisis began in the early 1990s when the World Bank invested heavily in developing a coffee industry for Vietnam so that it too could have an exportable "cash crop." Since then, Vietnam has developed into the second-highest producer of coffee in the world. Unfortunately, the low-grade, Robusta bean coffee grown in Vietnam and other countries created a large surplus in the market. This surplus caused the wholesale price for Nicaraguan coffee—which is made mostly from higher-grade, harder-to-grow Arabica beans—to drop from around $3 a pound in 1996 to a low of 51 cents a pound. In Nicaragua, production costs were suddenly nearly double the selling price, and the price nose-dive resulted in massive unemployment and property foreclosure for many small-scale producers, who accounted for 64 percent of coffee production in Nicaragua at the time.

Nicaragua has never fully recovered from this crisis, and the fluctuating price of coffee continues to cause problems well into the new millennium. Between 1999 and 2001, coffee plummeted from $140 to just $50 a bushel. As a result, the Nicaraguan coffee supply has been unreliable and has lost considerable value in world markets.

But never fear, there is still hope! In 2004, *Coffee Review's* Kenneth Davids described Nicaraguan coffee as a poster child for what's gone wrong with coffee and named it the rising star of Central American coffee.

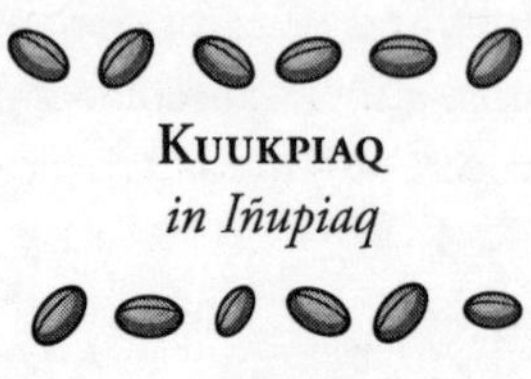

Kuukpiaq
in Iñupiaq

OTHER COFFEE-DRINKING COUNTRIES

Germany: Listen to the Music

If you love the atmosphere provided by traditional music and the kitsch of oompa music, then a table in a German *Kaffeekonditorei* may be the place for you. In Germany, the coffee and confectionery shops have small bands that play dance music from noon until well after midnight. Not only can you choose from coffee, tea and hot chocolate, but hungry patrons can also sample delicious pastries made in the great European tradition. In keeping with custom, the most beloved cafés play waltzes, fox trots, tangos and, of course, the tuba-trumpet-accordion music that has made Germany famous. It may make you think more of beer drinking and Oktoberfest than coffee and tarts, but either way, you are sure to enjoy yourself. Unlike Austrian cafés, however, in Germany one is expected to order at least one fresh cup of coffee every hour. Many waiters will simply serve café patrons a fresh cup every 60 minutes whether they have ordered it or not.

Greece

Throughout Greece, where it is customary that the eldest is served first, men and women of all ages consume a remarkable amount of strong coffee brewed Turkish-style. On the island of Corfu, for example, it is considered perfectly normal to consume over 20 cups of coffee every day. Whether on Corfu or in Athens, though, it is essential to remember that Greeks refer to their brew as "Greek" and not as Turkish. Any reference to "Turkish" coffee could get you in hot water since it will automatically be construed as a loaded political statement, showing preference to the Turks. And you thought you were just asking for a cup of coffee!

Eastern Europe

In nearly all of the Eastern European nations, coffee is considered an ideal after-dinner drink, especially when accompanied by a glass of *shlivovitz* (plum brandy) or sweet Tokay-style wine. In Russia, coffee is taken primarily with breakfast and after dinner and is almost invariably made by percolating. In Romania, Hungary, Poland, Slovakia and the Czech Republic, coffee houses are popular with members of both the working and intellectual classes. Even though instant coffee has become more acceptable in recent years, most Russians and those who inhabit the Balkan states think of it as a poor substitute for "the real thing."

Uganda

Uganda's primary export is coffee, and it is second only to Ethiopia as Africa's biggest coffee producer—Uganda, though, is the leading exporter of organic coffee in Africa. Ugandans have been known to mix green coffee beans with sweet grasses and various spices, dry them all together, and then wrap them in grass packets, which are then hung in homes to serve as both talismans and decorations.

Caribbean

One of the finest coffees in the world is the Blue Mountain variety that comes from the Caribbean island of Jamaica. Throughout the Caribbean, coffee is treated with great respect. Whether percolated or made with an espresso machine, it is considered traditional to drink coffee with a bit of lemon rind floating in the cup. While it is socially acceptable to add sugar, brandy or liqueur to one's coffee, adding milk at any time other than at breakfast is thought to be utterly barbaric.

THE BEST CITIES IN THE WORLD FOR COFFEE DRINKERS

Hidden Treasures

For most North Americans, coffee is simply a crutch for the sleep-deprived, but in some cities, it is a serious ritual, a way of life or—dare I say it?—a religious experience. So how far would you go for a cup of coffee? If you can't quite manage to hit every country to get a taste of their coffee traditions, how about hitting the trail with this top-five list of cities to visit in the quest for coffee nirvana? We're not going to bore you with the obvious: Seattle, Rome, sure...but how about someplace a little more off the beaten path?

Amsterdam, Netherlands

Okay, so it's not exactly off the beaten path, but Amsterdam is not necessarily known for its coffee, either. In Holland, tea is the

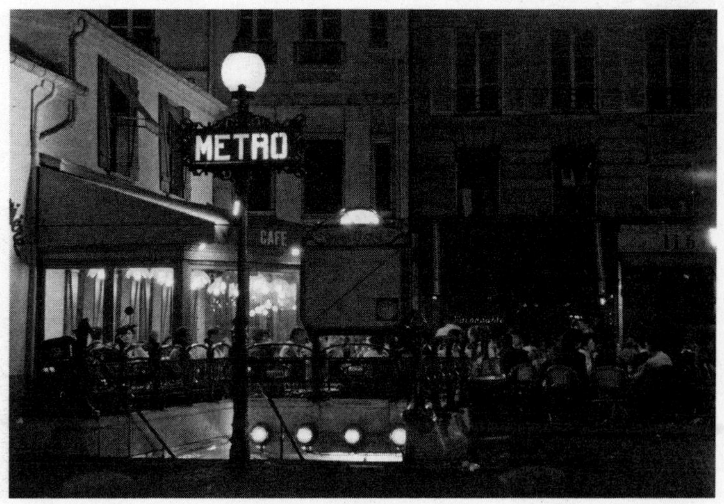

most-frequently drunk beverage at home, but when it's time to go out, the Dutch enjoy meeting with friends for a *gezellig* cup of coffee. *Gezellig* has no literal English translation, but implies coziness and familiarity. Since apartments are typically quite small in Amsterdam, it is more common to meet in the city's iconic *bruin* (brown) cafés. These coffee houses of the non-marijuana variety guarantee a little *gezelligheid* with friends and some good strong cups of coffee.

Melbourne, Australia

Local coffee culture is so entrenched in Australia's coffee capital that Starbucks simply can't make inroads. In 2008, Starbucks was forcer to close 16 of its Melbourne stores and countless others across Australia. After World War II, many Italian and Greek immigrants settled in Australia, bringing their coffee-brewing traditions with them, but since the 1980s, coffee culture here has really taken off. Locals agree that Brunswick Street in Fitzroy is Melbourne's go-to destination for some of the city's best coffee houses.

Wellington, New Zealand

Wellington is said to have more cafés per capita than New York City—an impressive fact considering that New York City has about twice the population of the entire country of New Zealand. In the 1950s, there was a wave of support for quality coffee houses as an alternative to beer-soaked rugby bars. There is no drip coffee to be found anywhere in this country. And, being a dairy nation, you will likely enjoy creamy milk in your "flat white." Or, if you're feeling adventurous, order a "tall black" and see what you get.

Buenos Aires, Argentina

You might think that Brazil would take the prize for the strongest coffee culture in South America, but the winner is actually Argentina. The concept of coffee-to-go is completely foreign in laidback Buenos Aires, where coffee drinkers prefer to enjoy their *café chicos* and *cortados* sitting in cafés and restaurants. And the best part of the ritual is that your coffee will likely be accompanied by an *alfajor*, a cookie sandwich with a dulce de leche center, also known as a "dream cookie."

Hanoi, Vietnam

You can practice on the plane: *Xin cho tôi mot cà phê sua da!*—"one milk coffee, please!" Sipped slowly through chips of ice, the strong, thick Vietnamese coffee is poured over an inch of sweetened condensed milk with a lidded metal filter perched on top. In essence, it is like having a little coffee pot right on top of your cup! Inside is a chamber for coffee and room for hot water. You will appreciate the ritual as you sit, wait and watch the coffee brew itself right over your glass. The whole process takes about 10 minutes, and the resulting drink is so sweet that some newcomers to Vietnam find it overwhelming. But taken properly, the mellow, caramel undertones make it wonderfully cooling on a hot summer afternoon. Once you've finished, you'll probably be offered a cup of green tea to cleanse the palate. Besides the standard four coffee drinks—*cà phê den nóng* (hot black coffee), *cà phê den da* (iced black coffee), *cà phê sua nóng* (hot coffee with milk) and *cà phê sua da* (iced coffee with milk)—all of which are available in any café—there is also *cà phê trung*, hot coffee with a raw egg beaten into it, with or without milk, which tastes a bit like a flavored meringue. With sugar, it is practically a meal. Hanoi is one of the only cities in Asia that takes its coffee so seriously, and some would even go so far as to say that Vietnam has a café culture to rival Italy's. You should go see for yourself.

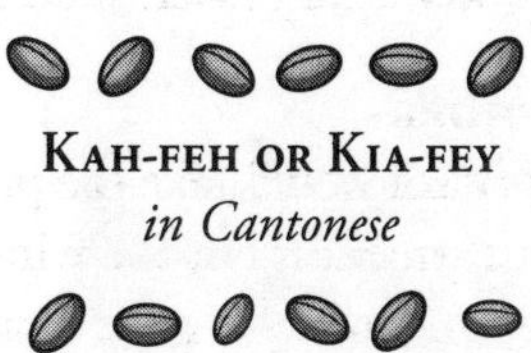

COWBOY COFFEE

Practice Makes Perfect

What lengths would you go to for your caffeine fix? Legend has it that cowboys made their coffee by putting the ground beans into a clean sock and plunging it in water heated over a campfire. Once ready, they would remove the sock and pour the coffee into tin cups to drink it.

Do you believe that story? Well, of course not. The truth is that "cowboy coffee" is a term used for no-muss coffee brewed in a standard cooking pot without any special devices, be it filters or socks. Because no special equipment is needed, it is ideal for campers, outlaws and those who travel light—and strong enough to put hair on your chest.

Water is boiled, ground coffee is added and the mixture is stirred. Once the grounds sink to the bottom, the coffee is ready. The coffee grounds tend to absorb a small amount of water while settling, so some recipes call for crushed eggshells or a raw egg (which is not consumed) to help separate the grounds from the coffee. One thing is for sure—it will keep you up long enough to ride off into the sunset with your cowpoke.

It also happens to be the most traditional method of coffee preparation in Finland, Norway and some Eastern European countries and is similar to Turkish coffee in style and preparation. Today, the French press replicates a similar process.

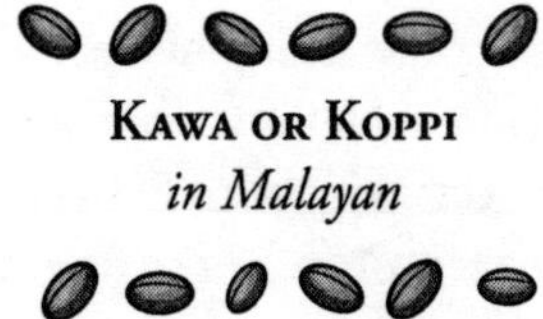

Kawa or Koppi
in Malayan

MARTINSON COFFEE: AN AMERICAN SUCCESS STORY

A Cup of Joe

Joe Martinson embarked on his coffee career at the age of 16. He began where every young and ambitious entrepreneur gets his start—in his mama's kitchen. Through trial and error, he developed an intricate and labor-intensive roasting process to bring out the best flavor in the beans. His special blend was unique because he roasted the coffee beans separately before blending them.

In 1898, Joe Martinson began selling his special roast from a push-cart on the streets of New York City. The aroma emanating from Joe's cart as he walked the neighborhood is said to have filled the air, and many believe this to be the origin of the expression "a cup of joe."

In 1908, Joe bought his first small factory and began marketing his premium blend to hotels and restaurants. Soon after, he packaged the ground coffee in cans and sold it to stores.

Coffee in a Rolls Royce

Believe it or not, Martinson eventually progressed to delivering his popular coffee in Rolls Royces! In a brilliant stroke of marketing genius, he bought a small fleet of Rolls Royces, removed the back seats and sent out his salesmen and deliverymen dressed as chauffeurs to deliver the coffee to premium hotels and restaurants in Manhattan.

As you can imagine, the company quickly took off. As author Marion Kane says, Martinson was ahead of his time and an excellent marketer: "The clever entrepreneur also used small airplanes to streak across the Big Apple skyline trailing banners and served free coffee on Wall Street in the thick of winter from a Martinson bus."

By the time Martinson died in 1949, he was top dog. In 2002, Mother Parkers, Canada's oldest coffee company and the largest family owned coffee and tea business in North America, purchased Martinson Coffee.

The Martinson warehouse would later become the Tribeca Grill, a favorite eating place of the rich and famous owned by stars such as Robert de Niro, Sean Penn and Mikhail Baryshnikov.

Coffee and Art

Although the Campbell's soup cans may be some of Andy Warhol's most recognizable art, did you know that he also did a similar art piece with Martinson Coffee cans? Warhol was obsessed with all things commercial and is well known for his iconic pop art. Warhol loved the mundane and ordinary things that made up everyday life and liked to explore and criticize mass media and consumerism. Art experts have said that "Martinson Coffee elevated an ordinary supermarket product to the realm of high art."

Wake Up and Smell the Coffee

Like most urban legends, there is no definitive proof that Joe Martinson coined the saying "wake up and smell the coffee," but it's a great story. As it turns out, the smell of roasted coffee is actually quite awful. It sounds lovely, the thought of waking up every morning to the smell of newly roasted coffee beans, but the odor of roasted coffee is very strong—some liken it to a charbroiled cigar. The problematic smell comes from the burning chaff, a waxy membrane on the coffee bean that emits the memorable odor. The smell of coffee that people enjoy comes from grinding it, not from roasting it. So if those in the neighborhood said anything along the lines of "a whiff of Joe," it likely wasn't meant as a compliment.

Navy Joe

Here are a few other theories about the origin of the expression "a cup of joe."

In 1914, the secretary of the U.S. Navy, Admiral Josephus Daniels, abolished the officers' wine mess. From that time on, the strongest drink aboard navy ships was coffee. It became the drink of choice by default and, over the years, was dubbed "a cup of joe" after the secretary. Daniels, not all bad, is also known for introducing women into the service and raising the standard of excellence in the Navy.

"A cup of joe" also refers to the GIs' favorite drink. During World War II, U.S. defense workers were supplied with as much coffee as they wanted. The slang was popular enough to be included in the Reserve Officer's Manual of 1931.

A variation on this theme has it that "Joe" refers to the average Joe, thus making "a cup of joe" the average drink of the average man. Others think that "joe" is just a sloppy way of pronouncing "java," which was a popular nickname for coffee in the 19th century. Yet another theory connects "a cup of joe" to the song "Old Black Joe," written by Stephen Collins Foster in 1860—however, this is unlikely since the lyrics have nothing to do with coffee.

The most prevalent theory of the origin of "a cup of joe" is the one that involves Josephus Daniels; this is the History Channel's preferred tale and the one that is most commonly retold, though there is still a strong case for Joe Martinson and his pushcart.

CAFFÈ
in Italian

QUICK AND DIRTY

You Know You're Drinking Too Much Coffee When…

1. You answer the door before people knock.
2. Juan Valdez named his donkey after you.
3. You ski uphill.

4. You get a speeding ticket even though you're parked.
5. You haven't blinked since the last lunar eclipse.
6. You just completed another sweater, but you don't know how to knit.
7. You grind your coffee beans in your mouth.
8. You sleep with your eyes open.
9. You have to watch videos in fast-forward.
10. The only time you're standing still is during an earthquake.
11. You can take a picture of yourself from 10 feet away without using the timer.
12. You're the employee of the month at the local coffee house, and you don't even work there.
13. You chew on other people's fingernails.
14. You're very popular in Mexico, where people use your hands to blend their margaritas.
15. You can type 60 words per minute with your toes.
16. All your kids are named "Joe."
17. You don't sweat, you percolate.
18. You walk 20 miles on your treadmill before you realize it's not even plugged in.
19. You forget to unwrap candy bars before eating them.
20. Charles Manson thinks you need to calm down.
21. You've built a miniature city out of little plastic stir sticks.
22. You're so wired, you pick up AM radio stations.
23. People test their batteries in your ears.
24. You named your cats "Cream" and "Sugar."
25. Your lips are permanently stuck in the sipping position.
26. You introduce your spouse as your "coffeemate."
27. You have a picture of your coffee mug on your coffee mug.

Real Groaners

 Be a coffee-drinking individual…espresso yourself!

 Man does not live by coffee alone—have a danish!

 Déjà brew: the feeling that you've had this coffee before.

- I'm on a low-fat, high stress diet—just coffee and fingernails.
- Captain Picard always drank tea; Kirk always drank coffee. Any questions?
- Inoculatte: to take coffee intravenously when you are running late.
- A morning without coffee is like sleep.
- A morning without coffee is like something without… something else.
- Goth and emo clubs should serve coffee—ice-cold coffee with nails and broken glass called "depressos."
- Ambidextrose: able to put sugar in coffee with either hand.

Trivia

- Coffee is the second most traded commodity after oil.
- It takes an average of 42 coffee beans to make an espresso.
- There are an estimated three trillion coffee trees worldwide.
- Forty-four percent of Latin America's cropland is used to grow coffee.
- The average daily wage on coffee plantations in Tanzania is $1.
- Seventy percent of all coffee is produced by smallholder farmers.
- Twenty-five million people are employed in the coffee industry worldwide.
- The global coffee industry is worth $10 billion.
- Caffeine is toxic and highly lethal to frogs.

COFFEE HOLIDAYS

Of course, coffee could hardly be a national obsession if it wasn't marked with a few holidays. No matter where you are, there are plenty of occasions to raise a cup in honor of the lifeblood that keeps us all going. No doubt there are some who celebrate National Coffee Day every morning.

In the U.S.

- January 25 is National Irish Coffee Day.
- February 17 is National Cafe au Lait Day.
- April 7 is National Coffee Cake Day.
- July 26 is National Coffee Milkshake Day.
- September 6 is National Coffee Ice Cream Day.
- September 29 is National Coffee Day.
- November 24 is National Espresso Day.
- December 26 is Coffee Percolator Day.

Around the World

- May 24 is National Coffee Day in Brazil.
- September 12 is National Coffee Day in Costa Rica.
- September 19 is National Coffee Day in Ireland.
- October 1 is the National Coffee Day in Japan.

WORLD'S MOST EXPENSIVE CUP OF COFFEE

The Straight Poop on Kopi Luwak Coffee

Someone in a bad mood might be asked the question, "Who pooped in your cornflakes?" But have you seriously ever been asked the question, "Who pooped in your coffee?"

The most expensive coffee in the world is the highly prized Kopi Luwak, produced with the help of the toddy cat, a small, nocturnal animal that lives on the island of Java. Also known as the Asian palm civet, the toddy cat eats fresh coffee berries along with other exotic fruits like mangoes and rambutans and drinks the naturally alcoholic tree sap used to make palm wine. What a life!

The coffee beans run through the cat's digestive tract and a natural fermentation is believed to take place. The beans are gathered when the seeds, still coated in some cherry mucilage, are eliminated in the cat's feces, giving a new definition to the term "hot toddy." Because it eats only the freshest and ripest berries, the toddy cat's droppings—after being thoroughly washed, of course—produce what many say is the world's finest coffee. Once roasted, Kopi Luwak can be sold to coffee connoisseurs for as much as US$400 a pound, though prices do vary.

Yes, that's right—the "best coffee in the world" is picked out of what is essentially cat poop. Japan is the largest importer, but it is also available in the United States.

Kopi Luwak coffee made a cameo appearance in the 2007 film *The Bucket List*, starring Jack Nicholson and Morgan Freeman. After tasting it, Jack Nicholson raves about the rare and delicious Kopi Luwak coffee and his character's lack of knowledge surrounding the beans' origins makes him…er…the butt of the joke.

COFFEE INFLUENCED

Nancy Astor: "If I were your wife, I would put poison in your coffee."
Sir Winston Churchill: "And if I were your husband, I would drink it."

Greensleeves

Lots of consumers love treating themselves to coffee but hate all the waste generated from a cup and sleeve, the cardboard cover used to help hold your coffee without burning your hands. Obviously, one eco-friendly alternative is to carry a reusable coffee mug, but what if you forget? Well, now there are reusable cup sleeves that can be easily stored in your car or purse. As an alternative to the wasteful paperboard sleeves that are offered at most coffee shops, these are original, practical and inexpensive. Made from burlap and green-produced felt, the sleeves cost $2.00 plus shipping and handling. They also come in a number of colors and designs and are handmade by an artist in the United States.

Coffee-Friendly Printers

If you like the smell of coffee in the morning, then the new coffee printer might be perfect for you. That's right—the coffee printer. Does it brew and print at the same time? No, but this eco-friendly printer, still just a design concept, purports to be able to turn leftover coffee grounds into a sustainable source of ink for your printer. Ink cartridges are notoriously costly to buy or refill, can stain your hands if mishandled and are decidedly unfriendly to the environment.

Not a coffee drinker—no problem. The RITI printer is designed to use tea dregs too. So how does it work? Simply place the beverage remains into an ink case on the top of the printer, insert a piece of paper and move the ink case left and right to print the image. The dregs should theoretically print onto the paper just like ink.

Admittedly, though it sounds like a great idea, this recent entry into the Greener Gadgets Design Competition still has a few flaws. The printer would be manually operated, which means you would have to move the cartridge back and forth with your hand. The action is slow and could definitely be improved. Although it doesn't require a power source—which I guess makes it handy if you have to print important documents in a blackout—it makes it impractical for everyday office use or for printing large documents. But it does mark progress towards energy-saving and innovative ideas as well as environmentally friendly alternatives. That, and your paperwork never smelled so good.

Which only leaves one question: who wants a refill?

Coffee in Song

Here are just a few examples of artists who have given coffee a sweet serenade:

- Bob Dylan, "One More Cup of Coffee"
- Emmett Miller, "You're the Cream in My Coffee"
- The Boswell Sisters, "Coffee in the Morning and Kisses in the Night"
- Jaybird Coleman, "Coffee Grinder Blues"
- Serge Gainsbourg, "Couleur Cafe"
- J.S. Bach, "*Ei, Wie Schmeckt*" (from the *Kaffeekantata*)
- The Ink Spots, "Java Jive"
- Tom T. Hall, "Don't Forget the Coffee Billy Joe"
- Lefty Frizzell, "Cigarettes and Coffee Blues"
- Lightnin' Hopkins, "Coffee Blues"

- Peggy Lee, "Black Coffee"
- Squeeze, "Black Coffee in Bed"
- Duke Ellington, "Cafe au Lait"
- MC Lyte, "Cappuccino"
- Blur, "Coffee & TV"
- The White Stripes, "One More Cup of Coffee"

COFFEE BEAN

In the 1995 award-winning film *The Usual Suspects*, starring Kevin Spacey, Benicio Del Toro and Gabriel Byrne, the bottom of a coffee cup takes on paramount importance. When Detective Kujan sees the "Kobayashi" logo on the bottom of his coffee cup, he realizes that Verbal Kint has made his whole story up.

Cigarettes and coffee, man, that's a combination.
–Iggy Pop, talking to Tom Waits

Coffee and Cigarettes in Film

Jim Jarmusch spent 13 years shooting short films on the side of his feature film projects, dragging actors aside and putting them in small scenarios for a film he would eventually call *Coffee and Cigarettes*. The film stars, among others, Iggy Pop, Tom Waits, Cate Blanchett, Bill Murray, Steve Buscemi, Steven Wright, The White Stripes, RZA and GZA from the Wu Tang Clan, Steve Coogan and Alfred Molina, and has some truly memorable scenes in an ode to the good stuff.

DID YOU KNOW?

One report suggests that part of the reason smokers consume so much caffeine is because it enhances the euphoric effects of nicotine.

Coffee and Cigarettes in the Grocery Store

I think we could all agree that many amazing joint-marketing opportunities are squandered because of a strange corporate squeamishness that ignores the sordid truth of how the population really consumes their products. For example, why haven't Trojan and Taster's Choice teamed up for a "would you like to come in for coffee" campaign? And why isn't skiing equipment sold along with a case of beer?

But maybe one of the most blatant examples of denial arises from the supposed gulf between coffee and cigarettes. They go together like cupcakes and icing—no doubt about it.

But in Japan, where the politically incorrect cup runneth over, they have shamelessly united these two together at long last. Yes, AM-PM, a Japanese convenience store chain, has started selling combo packs of Marlboro cigarettes with a can of Georgia Emblem Black coffee, the leading coffee brand of Coca-Cola Japan. Not exactly the squeaky-clean image the firm from Atlanta would want to be associated with in America, but hey, if it works in Japan…

I picture ripple chips and marijuana next, as the ultimate "joint venture."

Kafe
in Cambodian

COFFEE ADDICTION

Coffee: Intoxicating, addictive and perfectly legal.
–Unknown

Pros and Cons

Hot arguments about the health benefits versus the negative effects of coffee are very common these days. Some think that drinking it may prolong your life, others say it will shorten it, and many allege not to be able to live or function without it.

Caffeine is a central nervous system stimulant that temporarily wards off drowsiness and restores alertness. And while it's true that, in moderation, caffeine can increase the body's capacity for mental or physical labor, when used in excess, it can be intoxicating and cause nervousness, irritability, anxiety, muscle twitching, insomnia, headaches, gastritis and heart palpitations.

It has also been blamed for decreasing breast size, causing impotence and bringing on hallucinations. That doesn't seem to deter very many people, though, since some 90 percent of North Americans consume some form of caffeine every single day. As such, it is easily the world's most widely used drug.

While most of us have no firsthand tales of robbing a liquor store, shivering in a gutter or swan-diving into the worst toilet in Scotland (*à la Trainspotting*) just to score our next fix, make no mistake—coffee is highly-addictive. Regular consumption of coffee can result in the nervous system being unable to work without caffeine.

The Top Five Things You Probably Didn't Know About Caffeine

 Females can break down caffeine 25 percent faster than males.

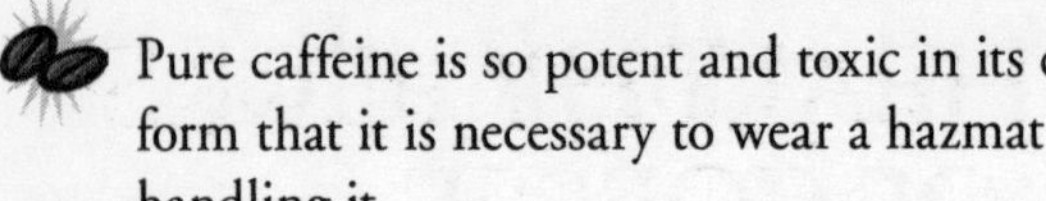

- Pure caffeine is so potent and toxic in its crystallized form that it is necessary to wear a hazmat suit before handling it.
- The effects of various psychoactive drugs were conducted on the web-weaving abilities of the common house spider. Out of the four drugs tested—marijuana, benzedrine, caffeine and chloral hydrate—caffeine caused the most serious impairment.
- Drinking coffee does not actually sober up a person who has been drinking alcohol—sorry to all you binge-drinkers out there, but the notion that coffee counteracts drunkenness has little truth to it. Coffee only makes someone who is drunk feel more alert, but actually reduces the rate at which alcohol is removed from the bloodstream.
- Caffeine is completely absorbed by the stomach and small intestine within 45 minutes of ingestion. Special studies conducted on the human body revealed that the body absorbs up to about 300 milligrams of caffeine at a given time, which is about four cups' worth. Any more will be excreted by the body and have no further stimulating effects.

THE HEALTHY PERKS OF COFFEE

But it's not all bad news. A cup of coffee a day…keeps the doctor away? Coffee has gotten a bad rap all these years—it turns out that, in some ways, coffee can actually improve our health, helping us to see the perks in the dregs at the bottom of our cups.

A Fluid Discussion

One of the biggest strikes against coffee is that it dehydrates you. It turns out that this isn't true at all. For years, health and exercise experts claimed that coffee and other caffeinated beverages caused bodily dehydration and therefore didn't count as a source of fluid in one's diet. We now know that there is no scientific evidence to support these views. In fact, caffeine is no more a diuretic than water and, while increasing urination, it does not increase the amount of fluid passed any more than drinking plain water would. So drink away!

A Source of Antioxidants

Antioxidants help defend our bodies from cell damage caused by free radicals and protect the body from diseases such as cancer, heart disease, diabetes and strokes. Trigonelline, the antioxidant that gives coffee its distinct taste and aroma, may even help prevent cavities by preventing bacteria growth on teeth! Coffee is also a good source of essential nutrients such as chromium, magnesium, niacin and potassium. In fact, a new study by researchers at the University of Scranton has revealed that coffee is America's number-one source of antioxidants, with black tea placing second and bananas third.

Simply the Best?

So does being the number-one source mean that it is the best source? Well, no. It is the equivalent of white bread being the

number one source of fiber—there are certainly better sources of fiber, just as there are better sources of antioxidants, but white bread and coffee are consumed the most.

DID YOU KNOW?

Caffeine is not what gives coffee its bitter taste. Only about 15 percent of the bitterness comes from caffeine; the rest comes from the antioxidants found in roasted coffee beans. Roasting is the key factor to bitterness. The darker the coffee is roasted, the harsher it tends to taste.

Coffee Boosts Brain Power

Researchers have determined that drinking just one to two cups of coffee per day may improve cognitive performance, including short-term memory and open-mindedness. Try telling that to your wife.

Coffee Improves Mental Health

Apparently, coffee is also a feel-good drug. The caffeine in the drink, by improving alertness and performance, helps to improve one's overall mood. A study of the relationship between coffee consumption and suicide rates among female nurses revealed that coffee drinkers had lower age-adjusted risks of suicide. Researchers have yet to determine whether the suicide rate is lower because coffee elevates one's mood or because it prevents depression, but it's clear nonetheless that coffee has a noticeably positive effect on the mental health of its drinkers—or maybe they're just too focused on where they're going to get their next caffeine fix.

If it wasn't for coffee, I'd have no discernible personality at all.

–David Letterman

Not Tonight Honey, I Have a Headache

Did you know that coffee is even good for headaches? The average eight-ounce cup of joe contains approximately 85 milligrams of caffeine—nearly the same amount as many oft-used headache medicines. A single dose of an over-the-counter pain reliever such as Advil or Excedrin contains up to 120 milligrams. The caffeine in the pill helps your body to absorb aspirin, ibuprofen and acetaminophen more quickly, meaning you don't need to take as much medication to feel relief.

Coffee Reduces Health Risks

Coffee contains several compounds that are known to affect human body chemistry and can reduce a myriad of health risks. For examples, studies have shown that coffee lovers may be at lower risk of developing type-2 diabetes—drinking coffee regularly may counter the disease's onset as coffee lowers blood sugar and promotes the quick delivery of insulin to the body's tissues.

And here's something even more stunning—coffee drinking may lower your risk of developing Alzheimer's disease or other forms of dementia. Dr. Miia Kivipelto, an associate professor of neurology at the Karolinska Institute in Stockholm, suggests several possibilities for why coffee might reduce the risk of dementia later in life. First, earlier studies linked coffee consumption with a decreased risk of type-2 diabetes, which has been associated with the onset of dementia. Secondly, in animal studies, caffeine has been shown to reduce the formation of amyloid plaques in the brain, one of the hallmarks of Alzheimer's disease. Finally, coffee may have an antioxidant effect in the bloodstream, thereby reducing vascular risk factors for dementia.

Parkinson's Disease

Coffee drinking may also lower your risk of developing Parkinson's disease as well as certain types of cancer. Regular coffee drinkers are up to 80 percent less likely to develop Parkinson's and half as likely to get liver cancer as those who don't drink it at all.

Parkinson's disease, a neurological disorder brought to national attention by such celebrities as Muhammad Ali and Michael J. Fox, is characterized by muscular tremors, slow movement and bodily weakness—a result of dopamine deficiency. Dopamine acts as the messenger between nerve cells. It is thought that perhaps antioxidant-rich coffee somehow helps slow down this degenerative process.

One study conducted in Japan found that those who did not drink coffee were three times more likely to develop Parkinson's disease. A similar study at the Harvard School of Public Health, involving approximately 135,000 people of mixed demographics, demonstrated that men who drank four to five cups of coffee daily cut their risk of developing Parkinson's almost in half. And sorry to all the ladies out there—so far, no studies have been conducted to see if the same holds true for women.

Coffee is so good for you that it can actually counteract the effects of excessive smoking and drinking. Research indicates that drinking coffee cuts the risk of alcoholic cirrhosis and heart disease. In fact, studies show that drinking three to four cups of coffee a day can lead to an 80 percent reduction in risk for cirrhosis of the liver, compared with non-coffee drinkers.

So who knows? Maybe the next time you go for a checkup, your doctor will prescribe you a cup of coffee just like in the olden days.

THE DOWNSIDE OF COFFEE DRINKING

Coffee Makes Your Breasts Smaller

Swedish scientists recently announced a reason why coffee should not be overly consumed by young adolescent ladies in particular—the number of cups you drink may negatively affect the size of cup you wear. The medical team at Lund University was doing cancer research about coffee's cancer-fighting properties when they discovered that coffee prevents the female body from developing breasts at a normal rate.

They discovered a statistically significant correlation between the consumption of more than three cups of coffee per day during adolescence and breast-cup size. In a cruel and ironic twist of fate, scientists also discovered in the same study that drinking three or more cups of coffee per day increases the chances of avoiding breast cancer and a rare form of heart cancer. So drinking more than three cups a day may make your breasts smaller, but it will prevent certain forms of cancer.

Hardly seems fair.

Caffeine Can Cause Hallucinations

Think the wild days of your youth are behind you? Think you have already sown all your wild oats? Well, think again. Yet another study claims that people who drink the equivalent of three cups of brewed coffee (or seven cups of instant) are more likely to hallucinate.

Yep. If you thought you were having breakfast with Jerry Garcia this morning, you may want to go and get yourself checked out. Seven cups of instant coffee contain a total of 315 milligrams of caffeine, according to data used by the researchers. That translates to about six cups of strong tea, nine colas, four Red Bulls or about one and a half cups of coffee at boutique cafés such as Starbucks.

Researchers at Durham University who have been studying the link between coffee and hallucinations say that their findings will contribute to the beginning of a better understanding of the effect that nutrition and diet have on hallucinations and other forms of psychotic behavior, such as delusions and schizophrenia. The scientists say that changes in food and drink consumption, including caffeine intake, could help people cope with or better prevent hallucinations.

Stress Inducer

Many factors are thought to be linked to caffeine-induced hallucinations, in part because of their impact on the body's reaction to stress. When under stress, the body releases a hormone called cortisol, and more of this hormone is released into the body when people have recently ingested caffeine.

Evidence on both sides of the coffee debate seems to be accumulating. Most people likely won't let scientific studies determine whether or not they drink a cup of morning coffee, but you have to admit that it is interesting to examine all of its effects on our bodies.

Coffee and the Olympics

If you have plans to become a world-class Olympian, you might want to consider leaving the coffee for the telemarketers and civil servants. In 2000, caffeine was officially banned by the International Olympic Committee, only to be allowed again in 2004.

Originally, athletes who tested positive for the equivalent of eight cups of coffee would have been banned from the Olympic Games, since that level could be construed as an effort on the part of the athlete to enhance his or her performance.

Why was it the ruling changed? Well, there has been further research indicating that caffeine concentrations higher than the allowable amount would actually *decrease* performance. But decreasing the threshold would risk banning athletes who only consume social amounts of caffeine, such as having a can of pop or a cup of coffee at breakfast. And since caffeine is metabolized at very different rates, it is possible that two athletes might consume the same amount of caffeine at the same time and incur different results—one passing, one failing.

The Great Caffeine Debate

Since the majority of us aren't Olympic athletes, it may not really matter, but if you train or exercise, you might want to know: does caffeine actually help or hinder?

There is ample research both supporting and naysaying coffee's effectiveness. On the plus side, caffeine is a stimulant and helps working muscles use fat as fuel, which will prolong the ability to exercise. It may also have an impact on the brain, tricking it into believing that the level of exertion is actually lower than it is, which increases stamina and allows athletes to push longer and harder. Other research has also shown that caffeine helps athletes to recover more quickly after strenuous exercise because it increases the muscle's stores of glycogen. This would be beneficial for say, triathalons, but not for a sport such as shotput or javelin, where a steady hand is required.

On the negative side, coffee brings with it more than a few undesirable side effects, including nausea, cramping, anxiety, fatigue and muscle tightness.

So if you are going to drink coffee, it is recommended to have a limited amount at least three to four hours before a race or any other physical exertion. If you want to increase caffeine's effectiveness and really push it up a notch, don't drink any coffee at all for a few days before the event, then down a cup or two on the big morning—that'll get you going!

BEAUTY TREATMENTS

Scrub Up and Smell the Coffee

Believe it or not, the coffee plant has healing properties. The cherry of the plant contains both moisturizing oils and antioxidant properties. Throughout the world, coffee has been used in various ways to improve skin condition, soothe irritations and revitalize cells. The essential oils found in coffee beans have the same 4.5 pH as our skin, so coffee works really well as an astringent to help keep the skin blemish free. And it also works as a sunscreen to protect the skin from UVA and UVB rays.

So does that mean splashing cold-brewed coffee on your face should become part of your morning ritual? Probably not, but the grounds can definitely do more than just perk you up in the morning.

Crushed beans are increasingly being used in body scrubs and massage oils at hotel spas. Get your caffeine fix at the same time as you exfoliate, tone, detoxify and refine your skin! Coffee acts as a free radical that helps defuse the oxidation reactions that destroy and prematurely age the skin.

Ground Arabica coffee is also used in a mud wrap as a therapeutic treatment designed to slough away dead skin cells and draw impurities and cellulite-inducing water from the skin. Yes, that's right—coffee helps break up the fatty deposits that cause cellulite. Alert the media!

Try This at Home

Used coffee grounds can help you get rid of cellulite. Mix one-quarter cup of warm, used coffee grounds with one tablespoon of olive oil. While standing over an old towel or newspaper, apply the mixture to your problem areas. Next, wrap the slathered areas with cling wrap and leave it on for several minutes, maybe while you brush your teeth or pluck your eyebrows.

Finally, unwind the plastic wrap, brush the loose grounds off your skin and then shower with warm water. For best results, repeat this procedure twice a week.

Spa Coffee

In 2007, the de Russie Wellness Zone—located in Rocco Forte's Hotel de Russie in Rome—launched a range of spa treatments using BodyCoffee products. BodyCoffee is a California company that takes its inspiration from Russia's famous Banyas, where bathers massage used coffee grounds onto their skin before hopping into a hot sauna, which speeds up the detoxifying process. Treatments range from anti-cellulite detoxifying body wraps and pedicures to a four-part BodyCoffee "Pure Bliss" treatment, and even include a post-treatment Pure Coffee Bliss cocktail at the Stravinskij Bar.

Pretty Woman

Julia Roberts reportedly can't get enough coffee scrub. The famous actress apparently loves the BodyCoffee Invigorating Body Polish. For the seriously addicted, other bestselling coffee-based products include everything from coffee body lotion to glycerin soap to JavaBalm for chapped lips.

Home Remedy

Well, you should've known it was coming. Coffee enema detoxification is a natural way washing away built-up toxins in your body, and, for all you do-it-yourselfers out there, this detoxification method can be done in the privacy of your own home. For it to be effective, though, you will need an organically grown, fully caffeinated brand of coffee that is specially made to be used in enemas. Because most commercial coffees are not made for this purpose (thankfully!), they are not likely to be effective.

So all you need is fresh organic coffee beans and a French press coffee pot. Add boiling water to the coffee grounds, which should be freshly ground, allow it to cool (obviously!) and, after separating

the coffee grounds from the liquid, pour the brewed coffee into your enema bag and from there follow the instructions provided with your enema kit.

You can buy enema kits?

Well, now you know. And I bet you'll never look at a French press the same way ever again.

COFFEE PROMISCUITY

Some people believe in Love, Peace and Soul. I, however, believe in Caffeine, Sex and Rock and Roll; If it doesn't make my ears bleed, give me a buzz or scream my name, I don't give a f%#!*

–Byron A. McIsaac

Science Made Me Do It

Ladies, good news—you may finally be able to convince your husband to splurge on that overpriced espresso machine you've been eyeing. In fact, coffee may be the new favorite gift next Valentine's Day since some recent studies have shown that caffeine may boost the female sex drive. But gentlemen, before you rush out to purchase a bean grinder, let's make it perfectly clear that, so far, the test has only been performed on rats. And researchers say that, in humans, coffee might only work to lift the libido among those who are not habitual users.

Scientists gave 108 female rats a moderate dose of caffeine. The caffeine shortened the amount of time it took the females to return to the males after round one of mating, indicating they were more motivated to "do it" again.

But here's the…er…rub—the rats had never been given caffeine before.

But the good news—other than being able to tell your partner that it's scientifically proven—is that the research could help scientists better understand sexual motivation and firmly determine which part of the brain controls sexual behavior.

In the 1700s, the Turks were big coffee drinkers, and the coffee prepared from the husk of the bean was much appreciated in the harems of the Turkish sultans.

Topless Coffee Shop
"Over 18 only—no cameras, no touching, cash only."

Hardly sounds like a sign you'd see outside a coffee shop. But indeed, in February 2009, the Grand View Topless Coffee Shop opened for business. Cup size has more than one meaning at this coffee house in Vassalboro, Maine.

The coffee shop caused quite a commotion among residents, who complained to local authorities; however, town officials said the coffee shop wasn't technically breaking any rules.

The most interesting and stunning piece of news, though, is *not* how many residents were understandably displeased, or that as many as 60 customers a day stop by, but rather that there were over 150 people who applied for only 10 available positions.

Seems like in a recession, you take what you can get…

Unfortunately, you'll have to cancel that road trip you just started planning in your head. In June 2009, only four months after it opened, the coffee shop was destroyed by arson. Luckily, it happened after hours and no one was injured, but unluckily, no topless employees could be seen fleeing the scene.

The influence of coffee in stimulating the genital organs is notorious.

–Dr. John Harvey Kellogg (1877)

The Original Viagra

Men have been searching since the dawn of time for a natural aphrodisiac that will turn them into sexual superheroes in the bedroom—everything from sea slugs to hippopotamus snouts to beheaded male partridges have actually been used in past attempts to increase sexual function. It turns out that they didn't have to look any farther than their coffee percolator.

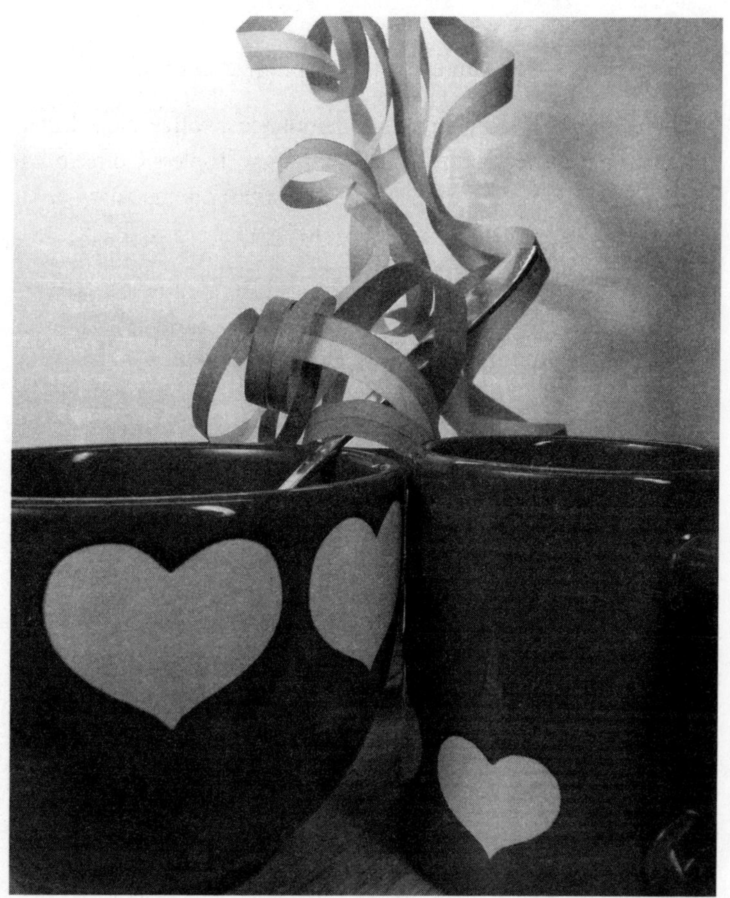

According to a *Men's Health* article, your morning cup of coffee might be "perking" you up in more than one way—men and women who have at least one cup of coffee a day are nearly twice as likely to describe themselves as sexually active, based on the undoubtedly in-depth study.

And guys who indulge in coffee everyday report fewer problems with erections. According to recent research from a university in the U.S., most of coffee's erotic potential can be chalked up to the java jolt. If you feel sluggish and the caffeine wakes you up, then you are more likely to be in the mood. Coffee in bed in the mornings is the idea, but practice moderation—with the coffee, that is. Once you move beyond one or two cups a day, caffeine can leave you agitated and edgy, which is definitely not a turn-on.

Sexy Seniors

The same goes for seniors. If your grandmother is a coffee drinker, chances are she's also a happy camper. In a study done by biopsychiatrists on sexual functioning, it was found that among the elderly who consumed at least one cup of coffee per day, the women had significantly higher rates of sexual activity and the men demonstrated an increased potency rate.

Good communication is as stimulating as black coffee, and just as hard to sleep after.
–Anne Morrow Lindbergh, American author and aviatrix (1906–2001)

Just for Fun

In 2001, an independently conducted national survey discovered just how seriously consumers are committed to their morning cup of coffee.

The survey asked: if you had to give up one of the following for an entire month, which would it be?

Coffee
Sex
Excuses
Internet access at home
Chocolate

Can you guess the results? Did coffee beat out sex? Thankfully, no—but it did place second only to sex on the priority list for both men and women. The majority of respondents said they would give up chocolate, excuses and the Internet—in that order—before they'd give up their morning cup of joe.

Women were twice as likely to forego Internet access as men. Men claimed, by a wide margin, that they'd give up excuses before they'd give up the Internet, though analysts are divided on whether this measures their commitment or their honesty.

Respondents for the survey were qualified as adult coffee drinkers who like chocolate and regularly have Internet access at home.

Coffee Is Better Than Sex

We all know that "coffee" is a big dating double entendre, as in "Would you like to come in for *coffee*?" It doesn't mean the same thing as "Would you like to come in for *a cup of coffee*?"

Many people might think the two questions are interchangeable, but they're wrong and woefully uninformed—a "cup of coffee" means a cup of coffee, whereas "coffee" means sex.

Kave
in Yiddish

TOP 10 REASONS WHY A CUP OF COFFEE IS BETTER THAN SEX

10. You can make coffee last as long as you want.
9. Coffee never has a headache.
8. A cappuccino is a guarantee of good head.
7. You can always start the day with good coffee.
6. Drinking coffee on your own doesn't make you feel sad and pathetic.
5. You don't get into trouble for having coffee in front of your parents.
4. There's no moral or ethical dilemma in paying for coffee.
3. A cup of coffee never complains if you want more.
2. It is possible to drink a cup of coffee even when you're really tanked.
1. You can light up a cigarette halfway through a cup of coffee.

Kaffe
in Danish

FAIR TRADE

Coffee Inflation

There is a lot of conflicting information about sustainable coffee growing and, by and large, consumers are either uninformed or confused about the impact these practices can have on the industry.

The fair trade movement is aimed at redistributing profits so that farmers receive a decent wage for their hard work. Nearly seven million tons of green coffee beans are produced each year worldwide and the majority of those are handpicked. Coffee farmers earn as little as four cents per pound for these handpicked beans, and for every pound of gourmet coffee sold, smallholder coffee farmers earn just over twelve cents.

According to a 2002 Oxfam report, Third World families dependent on money generated from coffee sales are being forced to pull their children out of school, especially young girls. The families can't afford basic medicine and are even cutting back on food. Coffee traders are also going out of business and national economies are suffering, with some banks collapsing. Government funds are being squeezed dry, which puts pressure on health and education and pushes governments further into debt.

The five largest Western coffee roasters are Nestlé, Sara Lee, Kraft, Proctor & Gamble and Tchibo. They have been accused of encouraging the overproduction of coffee, engineering a catastrophic fall in prices for coffee growers in Third World countries. Since 2000, prices have fallen to historically low levels—Oxfam reports that over 25 million coffee producers have been forced into dire poverty. Meanwhile, Western consumers still pay exorbitantly high prices for their drinks in gourmet coffee-bar chains, with none of that money going back to the people who provided the coffee beans in the first place.

Low-grade Beans Flooding the Market

The oversupply problem created by countries such as Vietnam is exacerbated by the increased frequency of defective coffee beans and foreign matter in coffee mixtures as more low-quality coffee enters the market. Traditionally, coffee producers would meticulously remove foreign matter and bean defects before exporting their coffee; today, cost cutting has resulted in having fewer employees around to remove the stinkers. Even more problematic is the sale of these defective beans for extra money—known in the trade as "triage"—to roasters who then use them in their coffee blends.

In fact, the quality of coffee in the U.S. market has become so low that imports destined for low-end blends often contain defective coffee beans such as blacks, foxes, sours and under-ripe or over-fermented beans. Arabica producers are essentially being required to compete on price against substances that would not have been able to be sold as coffee 10 to 20 years ago. Furthermore, the sheer quantity of low-quality coffee imports has frustrated overall efforts to promote more coffee consumption. Simply put, it is very difficult to persuade people to drink more coffee when so much of the coffee on the market is substandard.

Starbucks is the largest international purveyor of fair trade coffee, importing 18 million pounds in 2006.

Nueva Alianza, Guatemala

In the summer of 2007, I spent two weeks volunteering on a cooperative coffee farm in Guatemala called Nueva Alianza. I was devastated to discover that fair trade coffee is not the knight in shining armor it is portrayed as to java guzzlers in the industrialized world. Fair trade coffee is something of a mixed bag.

In order to be fair trade certified, coffee producers must pay €2000 (roughly $3000) to purchase a coffee license and must also meet certain standards set by the Fairtrade Labelling Organizations International, or FLO. This is a good thing, since these standards ensure quality control and avoid abuse and corruption, but they are only valuable insofar as they actually improve the lives of the people they are meant to benefit.

The average Guatemalan coffee picker earns less than $1000 per year. For poor communities such as Nueva Alianza, a fair trade certification costs nearly triple the average income, a price that is simply beyond their means. On farms with relatively low annual production, the increased market price that fair trade coffee commands is unlikely to cover the annual expense the community pays for their fair trade license. It's something of a vicious cycle—they pay more to earn around the same, or less.

Coffee pickers in Nueva Alianza receive 25 quetzals (about $3) per 100 pounds of coffee cherries picked. Though Nueva Alianza is seeking outside assistance to gain fair trade certification, right now the cooperative can't afford to operate within the fair trade system.

Consumer Conscience

So should we turn our backs on fair trade coffee? Admittedly, prices are much lower in Guatemala. To compare, in 2001, growers in Kenya received the equivalent of 31 cents per pound of green coffee. The vast majority of coffee we buy comes from producers who are paid about 54 cents per pound of beans, and most fair trade farmers get about $1.25 per pound of coffee. Whatever its faults, in my opinion it's imperative to continue buying fair trade coffee—the positives, despite the disparity, outweigh the negatives. Our dollars have a voice, and it is important for us to build consumer demand for fair trade products, including everything from coffee to cotton to chocolate to bananas. There is really no excuse for North Americans to do otherwise.

Why? Even though buying fair trade products may not immediately equate to increased wages for the coffee pickers themselves, the producers do benefit. In Nueva Alianza's case, because the money will be reinvested into the community as a whole, it will benefit the workers in the long run. Eventually, these reinvestments will allow farmers to produce a higher-quality crop with a correspondingly higher price, which will result in higher wages for the pickers. The market war fought over the price of coffee will end as soon as enough cognizant consumers look at the plight of coffee producers and take a stand, putting their money where their lips are. You can make a huge difference with a small commitment to purchase fair trade.

I think the same thing every time I belly up to the counter—if the coffee pickers are spending hours on a humid, sweltering hillside, braving coral snakes and fire ants, breaking their backs for $3 to pick a 100-pound bag of cherries, surely I can spend at least that much more to help ensure they are getting a humane wage for their product.

Any way you slice it, under the conventional system the pickers and the harvesters draw the short end of the stick. While fair trade coffee may be imperfect, its shortcomings are nothing compared to the swindling committed on a regular basis by the large-market coffee companies.

If you choose to support coffee producers in Guatemala, you can find out more about buying fair trade from Café Conciencia (Coffee with a Conscience) at www.cafeconciencia.org. A full 100 percent of the proceeds from coffee sales go directly back to the worker-owned communities such as Nueva Alianza that grow, process, roast and package it. That way, the communities are earning over five times as much per pound of coffee than they would on the conventional market, and over three times as much as in the mainstream fair trade market. This is a true grassroots organization with prices that can't be beat. One pound of coffee costs roughly $10, and that includes shipping and handling.

Certified Organic

The certified organic program was originally meant to provide an alternative to modern-day evils such as monoculture, low wages, dependence on fossil fuel and industrial farming structures, but has been reincarnated by big-business operators. Many international

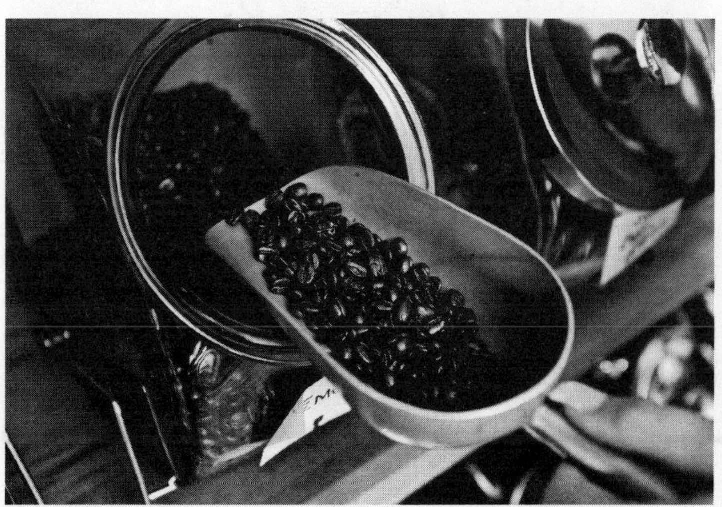

farmers don't have sufficient language skills to fill out the required paperwork, and large growing operations are steadily taking over the organics marketplace, eroding its profitability so that many producers can't afford the certification process.

There are still plenty of dedicated farmers who take pride in growing certified organic food and many more who have been farming organically for decades, but some have decided that the cost and the bureaucracy of being a certified organic grower is no longer worth it.

In this case, a quick and simple background check will let you know whether a coffee farm grows organic beans and whether or not they are officially certified. Doing your homework and getting to know the origin of your coffee as well as the story behind it will help you make a conscientious and informed decision.

To help you with your decision, the following two examples show how your dollars are making a positive difference in the lives of growers around the world.

SHADE GROWN IN DOI CHAANG, THAILAND

Love the Coffee, Love the Story Behind It

Doi Chaang coffee is made of 100 percent single estate, fair trade, organic, shade grown Arabica beans. What does that mean? It means it tastes good!

Unlike cheaper Robusta beans, which are grown at lower altitudes and exposed to the sun for accelerated growth, Doi Chaang's Arabica beans are carefully shade grown in high altitudes for four years. That means the coffee cherry takes longer to grow while the beans absorb the fragrance from neighboring pear, cherry and macadamia nut trees. The slow growth ensures the absorption of all the minerals and flavors, resulting in a berry that is naturally very low in caffeine with a more complex flavor. The beans are then handpicked, sun-dried and washed with fresh spring water.

Even better, Doi Chaang farmers earn at least 50 percent more than most fair trade farmers, roughly $2.28 per pound of green beans, in addition to getting 50 percent of all the profits from international coffee sales.

But that's not why you are going to love this coffee. You are going to love it because of the feel-good story behind it. The company's chairman, John M. Darch, is originally from Vancouver and has been living in Thailand for more than 25 years. Darch stumbled into the coffee business after meeting the Akha hillside tribe of Doi Chaang, which is now an 800-family cooperative in northern Thailand. The tribe was already growing coffee, and Darch and his partner Wayne Fallis were so impressed with the quality of the product that they were prompted to strike an unusually generous bargain with the Doi Chaang.

The Fairest of Them All

Rather than taking sole ownership of the farms and getting the beans at the cheapest price possible, Darch and Fallis made the tribespeople into business owners. The farmers own 100 percent of their growing and processing operations in Thailand, in addition to having 50 percent equity in the Canadian-based corporation. It is extremely rare, if not unheard of, for a coffee company to be grower-owned from crop cultivation to store shelves.

Darch took the green beans back to Canada and started an international company to get the word out, introducing the coffee to the world market. The first beans were roasted, shipped and cupped in April 2007, and the coffee has since catapulted to success.

In 2008, their medium roast was awarded 90 out of 100 by *Coffee Review's* Ken Davids, ranking them in the top five percent of medium roasts worldwide. The cooperative now also boasts a school, a coffee academy, fresh water, a medical centre and is now fair trade certified. Read more about them online at www.doichaangcoffee.com.

TAOFE
in Tahitian

WOMEN SUPPORTING WOMEN

Café Femenino

In 2004, world coffee sales amounted $56 billion in sales—less than $6 billion stayed in the countries of origin. That is a phenomenal imbalance. Another startling fact is that women coffee producers make up 30 percent of the 25 million Third World coffee growers that are responsible for producing nearly 75 percent of the world's coffee. Harsh gender inequality, poverty and abuse are rampant in most of these coffee-producing regions—many women coffee producers have no rights, no income and are sometimes abandoned by their husbands.

So Gay and Garth Smith decided to try and do something about it. They founded Café Femenino in 2004, a social program based in Peru for women coffee growers in rural communities throughout Bolivia, Colombia, Dominican Republic, Guatemala, Mexico and Peru. Café Femenino is changing the role of women in these remote rural coffee communities. More than 1500 women are currently active in the project, achieving self-empowerment, building social support networks and earning incomes through the production and sale of Café Femenino Coffee.

Café Femenino beans are touched by women every step of the way. The women must own the deed to the land to be doing the work. Café Femenino also provides training to women so they better understand the whole process of producing coffee, from growing and harvesting to roasting and marketing. More importantly, it gives them a loud voice where before they had none.

Pay It Forward

Normally, coffee roasters blend beans from different countries together and create their own names for these blends. What makes Café Femenino so unique is that roasters are asked to donate two percent of the profits from the sale of their coffee to a women's organization or back to the Café Femenino foundation itself—this ensures that a minimum of five cents per pound is donated by the roasters. This money has been used to send girls to school and to support other Third World coffee-growing regions, such as when the tsunami hit Sumatra.

Coffee roasters involved in selling Café Femenino coffee are also asked to commit to the project in the following ways:

- All sales contracts are signed by a woman in the company.
- A woman participates in the sales and marketing of the coffee.
- The name Café Femenino is used in the labeling of the coffee.
- The coffee is sold as a single-origin coffee to preserve the spirit of the project.

This circle of women supporting women is strengthening, inspiring and encouraging to witness. It is creating better working conditions and improving the household economy for women in the countries of origin. Coffee-roasting kitchens, for example, have improved ventilation and have raised the height of their stoves, to make the roasting easier on the workers' backs. Other profits are earmarked for better bathroom facilities, schoolbooks, higher-quality food for families, seeds to grow vegetables and more clothes for the children. This has brought stability to a large number of families and communities all across Central and South America.

Doesn't that just make you feel good all over? Bottom line: You can make a *huge* difference with just a small purchase of sustainable coffee.

COFFEE AND FOOD PAIRINGS

In General

In North America, most of us have a cup of coffee in the morning with breakfast and leave it at that. But in Europe and other parts of the world, coffee is an important and integral part of a meal, be it breakfast, lunch or dinner.

What to Drink with What You Eat authors Andrew Dornenburg and Karen Page give us some great tips on how to successfully and deliciously pair coffee with just about any food.

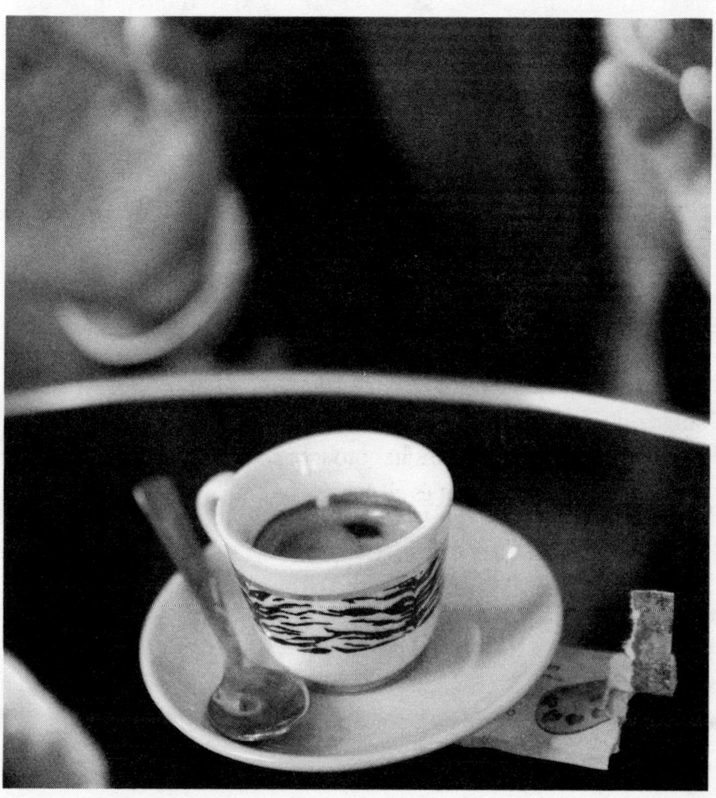

Coffee lovers with a sweet tooth will be glad to hear that coffee pairs exceptionally well with apple pies and tarts, chocolate desserts and—as the entire hungover world knows—any variation of breakfast or brunch dish, pancakes, waffles, toasts, cold pizza—or all of the above.

Specific Blends

Connoisseurs have even broken down specific beans to go with specific desserts. For example, African coffee such as Ethiopian—which produces lighter-bodied, milder coffees with floral and berry notes—goes well with chocolate and lemon desserts, but not with savory food. Asian blends—such as Indonesian, Java and Sumatran, which are big, bold coffees with lower acidity—are the ones you want to pair with savory food. Aged coffee—such as Sumatran Aged Mandheling, which often has a spicy flavor—complements bread pudding, pumpkin pie and spiced desserts. Central and Latin American blends, which tend to be more subtle and rounded with a crisp, clean acidity, are ideally paired with berries, biscotti, breakfast, carrot cake, cookies, doughnuts, lunch, muffins, nuts, nut bread and scones.

Dieters Beware!

Dark-roasted Italian, French and Vienna blends are green coffee beans that are heavily roasted, producing a "second crack" in the bean that releases its sugars for extra caramelization. This means that they taste bittersweet and have a low acidity, so they pair especially well with dark chocolate cake, ice cream and rich and creamy desserts—indulgence is not only allowed but encouraged!

This may come as a surprise to some, but French roast coffee pairs really well with roasted red and yellow peppers, especially with a little olive oil. Antipasto and biscotti will bring out the best in an Italian roast, while a Kenyan coffee will be happy to spend time in your mouth with lemon desserts, scones and freshly cut fruit.

If you have a light-roasted coffee—such as a mocha or Java, which has a bright, acidic, toasted grain taste—then berry desserts, freshly cut fruit and fruit desserts are the way to go.

Medium-roast coffees—such as Costa Rican, Guatemalan and Viennese, which are acidic and bright but lack the grain taste—will do better with cheesecake, custard desserts, lemon desserts and tiramisu.

If the thought of a hot coffee is making you sweat, then enjoying an iced coffee on a hot day may be the answer. Serving coffee on ice can kill some of the more subtle coffee flavors, so Willard "Dub" Hay, senior vice-president of Starbucks, recommends sticking with strong-flavored East African coffee such as Tanzanian or Kenyan for iced coffee and avoiding Sumatran or Guatemalan coffees.

A Roman drink called a *café correcto* is an espresso that has been "corrected," meaning that grappa or sambuca has been added to counteract the caffeine. Try it at the end of a meal with cookies.

Espresso and Biscotti: A Match Made in Heaven

In Italian *biscotti* simply means "biscuits," and the term may be used to refer to any sort of cookie. What we typically call "biscotti" is a very Americanized invention. In Italy, *cantucci di Prato* were the original biscotti, flavored with almond, served with *vin santo* and no longer than a chubby finger. *Cantucci* have been made in Italy for centuries, and they are considered a quintessential example of Italian cuisine.

Cantucci are made with slightly sweet dough that traditionally contains anise and nuts. First, the dough is baked in the shape of a loaf, then it is sliced, and the slices are baked for a second time. The second baking allows the cookies to become very crisp and crunchy. When the cookies are dipped in liquid, they become dense and chewy, absorbing the liquid along with its flavors, making them an ideal accompaniment for coffee and espresso. Cookies and tiramisu also taste excellent with a strong shot of espresso.

Coffee-flavored Food

If drinking coffee isn't your thing but you never met a dessert you didn't like, then you can take solace in the knowledge that coffee-flavored desserts can also be paired with any number of intriguing and unique beverages.

Banyuls, a dessert wine from France; any champagne, especially brut; coffee-flavored stout beer; and cocktails made with cognac or hazelnut liqueur, such as Frangelico, taste like a gift from the heavens with coffee-flavored desserts. Other possible pairings include port, both tawny and vintage, and sweet sherry.

Cheese And Coffee Pairings

Experimenting with adventurous cheeses may be the key to unlocking more coffee flavor. The longer the cheese is aged, the better it works, says food expert Jennifer Meier. Young *Gouda* pairs well with coffee because it is so mild, but aged *Gouda* offers sweet, caramelized flavors that not only stand up to but enhance the strongest cup of coffee. Or try *Piave*, an Italian cheese with a sweet flavor that can be described as a little bit fruity.

Take a cue from the Italians and serve ricotta cheese with espresso and biscotti—add fresh or dried fruit and a drizzle of honey to the ricotta, and you've got yourself a great meal.

The bite of a slightly sharp Cheddar matches the pleasantly bitter taste of coffee and espresso. Some Cheddars also tend to have nutty characteristics that further enhance the pairing.

Gjetost (pronounced "yay-toast") is a sweet Norwegian cheese. Serving it with coffee is much like serving dessert. The cheese is made by slowly cooking down whey until the milk sugars caramelize. *Gjetost* actually looks like a big square of caramel—and tastes like one, too—so it is a natural pairing with coffee.

If you have been sticking with old standbys like doughnuts and coffee, I do believe it may be time to try something a little more risqué.

THE MOST ORIGINAL IDEAS YOU NEVER THOUGHT OF FOR LEFTOVER COFFEE

While some of us may drink our coffeepots completely dry in the morning, there are just as many who always have some left over. So instead of wasting it, here are some really neat things to do that don't involve pouring it down your sink.

Coffee Ice Cubes

Want to know a secret? One of the key ingredients for making the best iced coffee at home is the coffee ice cube. Make the ice cubes with a batch of extra-strong coffee and keep them in Ziploc bags until you are ready. Use your coffee cubes instead of plain ice and eliminate the chance of ending up with watered-down iced coffee.

The World's Best Iced Coffee

Put equal parts espresso and milk (one long shot) into the blender and as much sugar as you like. Put on the lid, but remove the center hole. With the blender running at top speed, drop about four coffee ice cubes through the hole, one at a time. Continue blending until the mixture is smooth. Pour into a tall glass over plain ice. If that's not your style, adding a couple scoops of chocolate or vanilla ice cream will turn your iced coffee into a delectable mocha milkshake.

Bake a Mocha Dessert

Substitute equal amounts of coffee for the water in your chocolate cake or brownie recipes and easily turn chocolate recipes into mocha ones. You can also try soaking ladyfingers in coffee for extra-tasty tiramisu.

Chili and Beef Stews

Just like the dark chocolate trick, sneaking a teaspoon of ground coffee into chili will give it a unique and dynamite flavor. Also add some beer to the chili, and you'll have a recipe for cowpoke success.

Coffee Marinade

Mix leftover coffee with half the amount of good red wine and marinate a flank steak in it for 30 minutes before grilling, or make your own "Red Eye Sauce" by sautéeing a thick slab of ham in coffee.

Coffee Jelly

It may sound crazy, but you can make a really tasty coffee jelly by using the same proportions of liquid to gelatin on the Knox box, just substitute brewed coffee for water. The jelly is black and sweet and, when served with vanilla ice cream, it makes a really delicious eye-opener.

Coffee + Beans = Beautiful Music

Add some coffee to pinto beans and let sit for 15 minutes. The coffee deepens the flavor, adding a certain mystery to the beans. Or if you have more time, use coffee-soaked-pinto-bean broth instead of beef broth—soak the beans overnight, then cook them in water with onions, oregano, a pinch of herbs and salt. The deep color and scent are very inviting.

Salad Dressing

Finely ground raw cauliflower, grated Parmesan, mayo and sour cream thinned with a cup of coffee makes a phenomenal and unique salad dressing. Serve with robust greens like romaine or blanched vegetables and you're cookin'.

Water Your Plants

Acid-loving indoor or outdoor plants will thrive if you occasionally water them with cold coffee. If your coffee is too strong, dilute it with a little water. You can also use leftover coffee grounds, but please, no cream or sugar.

OKAY, BUT WHAT ABOUT COFFEE GROUNDS?

Other than brewed coffee, there is also a whole host of things that can be done with coffee grounds while reducing landfill waste at the same time. Does it get any better than this?

A Gardener's Delight

If your lawn is yellow or patchy in places, adding coffee grounds might just wake up your yawning grass. Coffee grounds are organic matter and act just like any fertilizer, adding nutrients to the soil. They will also turn your grass a richer green as the grass soaks up the coffee.

As with any ground shells or hulls, java beans can be worked into the soil to improve aeration and drainage. This is especially effective on neglected or compacted clay soil.

Ground espresso beans will also help loosen the soil, allowing for better absorption of air, water and nutrients. Ground beans, however, should not be used as mulch because they are so fine and can be blown away or can clump up and prevent absorption.

Good To The Last Crop

Used coffee grounds, on the other hand, make great mulch. Gardeners report that their trees, shrubs and flowers respond very well when mulched with coffee grounds. To maximize results, work the used coffee grounds into the soil before planting seeds. After your plants start to germinate, work in more coffee grounds near the plants. Used coffee grounds are said to repel snails and slugs in addition to adding vital nutrients to the soil.

You can also increase your carrot and radish harvest by mixing the seeds with dry coffee grounds before planting them and, finally, keep cats from using your garden as a litter box by spreading used coffee grounds and orange peels throughout your flowerbeds.

But Wait! There's More

Fourteen more things coffee grounds can do if you don't happen to be a gardener:

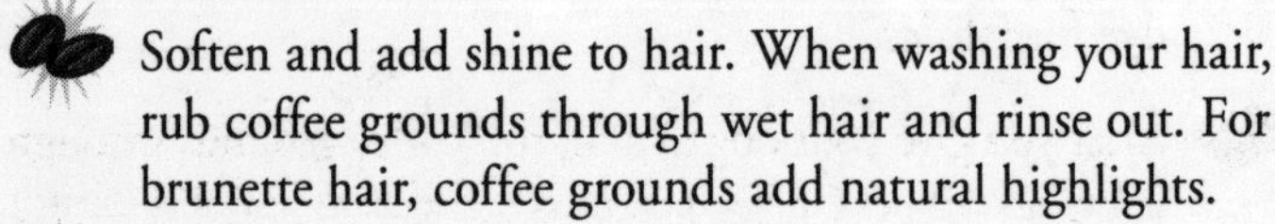

- Soften and add shine to hair. When washing your hair, rub coffee grounds through wet hair and rinse out. For brunette hair, coffee grounds add natural highlights.

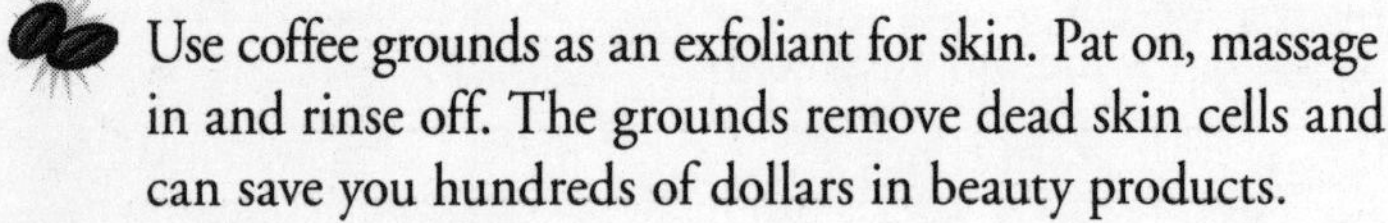

- Use coffee grounds as an exfoliant for skin. Pat on, massage in and rinse off. The grounds remove dead skin cells and can save you hundreds of dollars in beauty products.

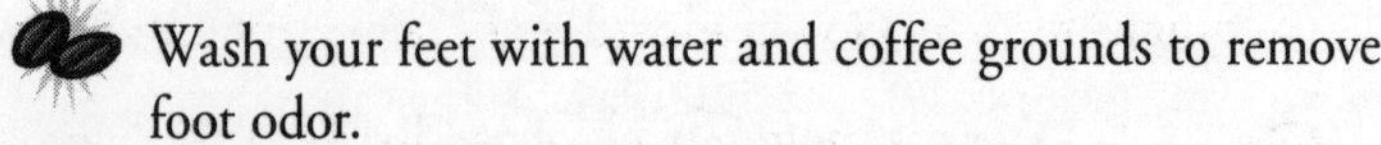

- Wash your feet with water and coffee grounds to remove foot odor.

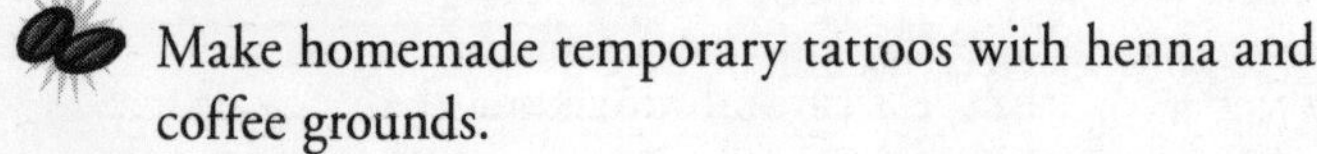

- Make homemade temporary tattoos with henna and coffee grounds.
- Use coffee grounds to repel ants. Rubbing coffee grounds into the infested area will make the ants, who don't like the smell, march away into somebody else's bathroom.
- Deodorize a freezer. Place a bowl with used coffee grounds in the freezer to remove unwanted odors. Add a few drops of vanilla to the grounds to absorb even more odor.
- Rub coffee grounds on your hands to get rid of smells from chopping pungent foods such as onions.
- Make a used-coffee-grounds sachet. Fill old nylons or cheesecloth with dry used coffee grounds and hang in your closet to absorb odors.

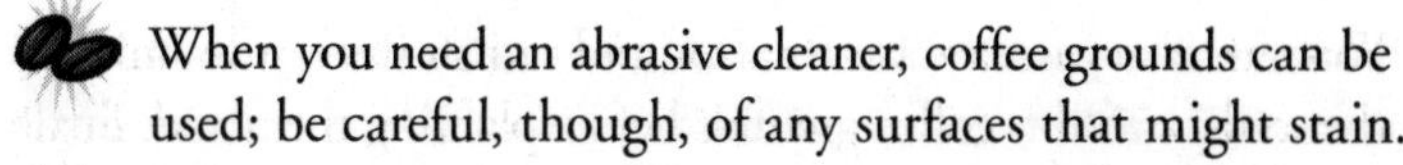

- When you need an abrasive cleaner, coffee grounds can be used; be careful, though, of any surfaces that might stain.
- Remove furniture scratches with wet coffee grounds.
- Got a fireplace? Cleaning it is a dusty, dirty job. But not if you sprinkle wet coffee grounds over the ashes first to hold them in place, making the dust clouds more manageable.
- Dye fabric, paper or Easter eggs. Simply add used coffee grounds to warm water and let sit for a bit to create a brown dye for fabrics.
- After you give your dog a bath, rub coffee grounds through your pet's coat. Coffee grounds are said to repel fleas.
- Grow mushrooms in old coffee grounds. Yep, you can bury fresh oyster mushrooms in a bucket of damp grounds, wait several weeks and harvest your own homegrown fungus for free. Go ahead and make some fresh soup.

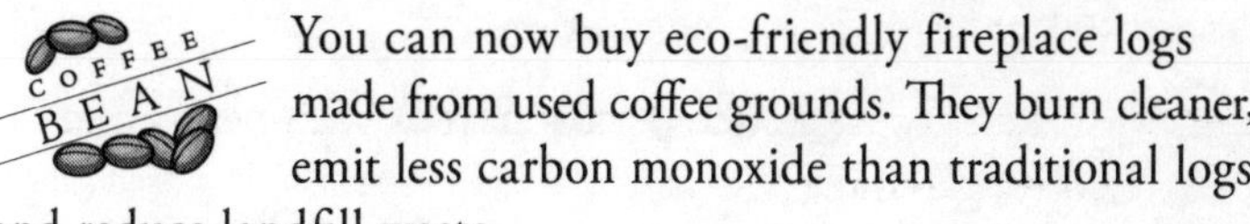

COFFEE BEAN

You can now buy eco-friendly fireplace logs made from used coffee grounds. They burn cleaner, emit less carbon monoxide than traditional logs and reduce landfill waste.

Grounds and Gas

And speaking of eco-friendly, did you know that used coffee grounds also make a pretty decent biofuel?

Although Brazil has been working with this technology for several years, it is relatively new in the United States. One barrier to greater biofuel use is the high cost of production. One of coffee's advantages is that it is high quality—spent coffee grounds retain around 11 to 20 percent of their essential oils—and low cost to produce. This compares well with other more common biofuels such as palm oil, rapeseed and soybean.

So of the 16 billion pounds of coffee beans grown annually, up to 340 million gallons of biodiesel could be made out of the coffee grounds that would otherwise end up in a landfill or on a compost heap.

Because coffee is jam-packed with so many antioxidants, coffee-fuel is actually more stable than some other biodiesels. Best of all, the fuel actually smells like coffee. Wouldn't that just make your morning commute a little bit more bearable?

All told, you could be heating your home, driving your car, scrubbing your face, shining your pets, scaring away ants and saving the environment with coffee! As if you needed a reason to like it any more than you already do.

Kafija
in Latvian

ABOUT THE AUTHOR

KAREN ROWE

Karen Rowe is the author of *For the Love of Chocolate* and has written for *The New West, MOMeo Magazine* and *The Calgary Herald's Q* blog. Her business, Front Rowe Seat, keeps her busy as a writing coach, ghost writer, editor and freelance writer. She currently lives in Calgary, Alberta, and is not ashamed to admit that she has never tasted an Ethiopian Yirgacheffe.

Her coffee of choice is Red Tail Dark Roast from Good Earth.

ABOUT THE ILLUSTRATOR

CRAIG HOWRIE

Craig is a self-taught artist who has known the author for longer than either of them would care to admit. His line art has been used in local businesses' private events as well as a local comic book art anthology. He is also a songwriter working feverishly on a project that will hopefully see the light of day within the next decade or so....